NEW YORK STATE
GRADE 5
ELEMENTARY-LEVEL
ENGLISH LANGUAGE
ARTS TEST

Hermon R. Card, M.Ed.

BARRON'S

All inquiries should be addressed to:
Barron's Educational Series, Inc.
250 Wireless Blvd.
Hauppauge, NY 11788
www.barronseduc.com

ISBN-13: 978-0-7641-3783-9
ISBN-10: 0-7641-3783-2

International Standard Serial No. 1937-0911
Printed and bound in the United States of America

9 8 7 6 5 4 3 2 1

Contents

Tips for Teachers and Parents

You are about to use a resource for preparing students to be successful on the New York State Grade 5 Elementary-Level English Language Arts Test. The following tips will serve as an introduction to the test and a guide for using this text.

- The exercises in this book are congruent with the New York State Core Curriculum and the Learning Standards of the New York State Education Department.
- By examining the expectations as they are published by NYSED, you should see that your school and classroom curriculum is a more than adequate background for success on this test.
- Utilizing the exercises in this book will prepare your students to take the test by familiarizing them with the structure, rules, and expectations of the test. Likewise, it will offer the opportunity for them to review the essential learning that has taken place in their K-5 classroom experience and in their daily use of the English language.
- The practice exercises are designed so that you might use them in whatever way best suits your instructional opportunities . . . either as an augmentation of your classroom activities, as part of a test preparation activity, or as material for focused review sessions.
- The practice exams are intended to be administered under the same time restrictions as the actual test,

but you may adjust the time allowed according to your schedule. You may certainly shorten the time allowed if necessary. This may actually have the beneficial effect of showing your students that they will have sufficient time to complete the actual ELA test.

- It is not advisable to assign the practice tests as homework or otherwise, since it diminishes the chance for students to understand the pace at which they should proceed on the test.

Preface

GETTING READY FOR THE TEST

Now that you have been introduced to the *New York State Grade 5 Elementary-Level English Language Arts Test* (ELA 5, from here on), you can begin preparing for it.

The ELA 5 test is in the same format as the ELA 3 test you took in third grade, but different from the ELA 4 test that you took last year. This chapter contains questions that were asked by some typical students taking the ELA 5 test in 2007. The answers should help you feel more confident when you take the test.

* *

Athletes and performers always practice before their events to reinforce the skills that they already have. Test takers also can expect to do better if they understand the "setup" of a test, the way it works. Just like the tests you take in school, this test follows a certain pattern. If you understand how a test is set up, you will better understand how to take the test.

NOTE: The answers to these questions are based on the 2006 and 2007 New York State ELA 5 Test, the only such tests administered so far. Because the test is based on testing models from past New York State Assessments, it is unlikely that the format will undergo any significant changes from year to year.

Why do I have to take this test?

All fifth graders in New York State schools are required to take the English Language Arts 5 Test. You must take the test in order for your school to know your level of achievement in relation to the New York State Learning Standards and the Grade 5 Core Curriculum. This will also help schools create programs that will improve your chances of success as a student of English Language Arts.

Is this test like the one we had last year?

Some parts are similar, but overall, it is a different type of test.

The test is similar in that there will be MULTIPLE-CHOICE questions in a READING section and in a LISTENING section.

The test is different in that you will **not** have the essay type questions that you had on the ELA Grade 4 test. Instead, you will have an EDITING exercise.

What will I have to know?

You will not be asked any questions that test your knowledge of specific facts. All answers to questions on the MULTIPLE-CHOICE sections (the reading and listening sections) are based on the information given in the passages and relate to how well you understand what you will have read and listened to.

What kind of questions will I be asked?

There are three types of questions on the test, and none of them are new to you.

MULTIPLE-CHOICE—You are familiar with MULTIPLE-CHOICE questions, questions where you are given a choice of four responses, one of which is the correct answer to the question you have been asked. You will be asked this type of question in both the reading and listening parts of the test.

SHORT RESPONSE—In the reading and listening parts of the test, you will be asked to answer a question with a short written response.

A SHORT RESPONSE question asks for a simple written response (usually in a sentence or two) to a question you will be asked. You will have one based on the reading passages on **Day One** and one on the listening passage that will be read to you on **Day Two**.

EDITING—You will read a paragraph and correct errors in grammar, usage, capitalization, and punctuation. You will not be responsible for correcting spelling errors.

In the EDITING question, you will be asked to correct mistakes in a short written passage. You had this same kind of question on the Grade 3 ELA test, and you are used to EDITING your own written work and helping your fellow students edit their work during writing conferences. This question really is just about finding mistakes and fixing them.

What else will I need to be able to do?

Even though there are no essay questions on this test, your writing skills are important. You must be able to write clear answers to the SHORT RESPONSE questions.

Your writing skills will also be important when you answer the EDITING question, where you will be correcting someone else's writing errors. Your listening and note taking skills will be important too. You will need to listen carefully and take good notes on the LISTENING section of the test.

How is the test set up?

The test is given on two days.

On **Day One**

- You will have MULTIPLE-CHOICE questions about passages that you read.
- You will also have a SHORT RESPONSE question on which you will write a short answer to a question based on one of the passages.

On **Day Two**

- You will have more MULTIPLE-CHOICE questions. These questions will be asked about a passage that will be read aloud to you.
- You will also have a SHORT RESPONSE question to which you will write a short answer based on the passage that is read to you.
- You will have an EDITING question that will require you to read a short paragraph and fix any errors you find.

What will the reading passages be like?

The passages will be the same type of reading that you do in your regular classes. They will be from a variety of types, such as articles, essays, poems, biographies, fables, and so on. They are designed to be on the reading level of a typical fifth grade student.

How many questions will be on the test?

On **Day One**, the reading portion of the test, there will be 21 questions, 20 MULTIPLE-CHOICE and one SHORT RESPONSE.

On **Day Two**, the listening section will have four MULTIPLE-CHOICE questions and one SHORT RESPONSE question. The EDITING portion of **Day Two** will be a written passage containing errors you must correct.

How long will the test take?

The test is given in two parts, one section on Day One and two sections on Day Two.

Day One:

You will have 40 minutes to read the passages and answer

■ 20 MULTIPLE-CHOICE questions and
■ One SHORT RESPONSE question

Day Two:

You will have 10 minutes to answer

■ Four MULTIPLE-CHOICE questions and one SHORT RESPONSE question AFTER the selection has been read to you twice.
■ You will have 10 minutes to correct the errors in the EDITING passage. (REMEMBER that you will have a practice EDITING exercise before the actual 10-minute test passage.)

Who scores my test?

Teachers and administrators score tests from your school and from other schools in your area. Representatives of the New York State Education Department train all scorers in the scoring process.

Scores are available after the tests have been scored, reviewed, and submitted to a process known as *standard setting*.

What if I "fail" the test?

The scores on the test are not categorized as passing or failing.

There are four scoring levels, all of which refer to the level at which you meet the New York State Learning Standards for ELA 5. They are *Meeting* (the standards) *with Distinction*, *Meeting*, *Partially Meeting*, and *Not Meeting*.

Students who are determined to be *Partially Meeting* the standards or *Not Meeting* the standards are not thought of as failing, but are considered eligible for Academic Intervention Services (AIS) provided by their school districts as part of the students' instructional schedule.

What effect will the test have on my class grade?

It will have no direct effect, since it is a state assessment test. Unlike New York State Regents Examinations, this test is not graded for the purpose of determining passing and failing grades, and it will not be given numerical or letter grades that relate to typical class grading systems. New York State Assessment Tests are not part of the regular curriculum grade. They are used to determine if students may need extra academic help through Academic Intervention Services to do well in ELA in the future.

Therefore, students who are mandated to receive such extra help will likely experience a higher degree of success in future classroom work (better grades) because of the beneficial effect of the AIS.

How can I study for the test?

This is not a fact-based test. It is a test to measure your skills in English Language Arts rather than to determine what you know. STUDYING has to do with learning, but actually, you have been "studying" for this test ever since you began reading, writing, listening, and speaking.

You probably will not need to learn new things, although you may pick up some helpful information during your class preparation for the test or through the exercises and review information in this book.

What about reviewing?

There is a difference between REVIEWING and STUDYING. For a test like this, REVIEWING is the key, since it is really a form of practicing the skills you have already developed to make them better, much like practicing for a baseball game or rehearsing for a band concert. You are actually practicing for the test all the time.

Usually, teachers will administer and discuss practice tests, and go over strategies for taking the test and answering certain types of questions. Practice tests will help you become familiar with what the actual test will be like. As far as practice goes, you have actually been practicing for this test ever since you began to use the English language.

How much time should I spend reviewing?

The better you have done in the classroom on a day-to-day basis, the less time you will need to spend actually reviewing for the ELA test.

Regardless of your achievement in class, your teacher will review the test and review the type of items and the skills necessary to do your best on the ELA assessment. This may take place during specific review classes or during your normal classroom time.

Be sure to participate actively in any review and practice sessions that are offered in class, because it will help you understand what the test is like. This will help you to be confident when you take the actual test.

You will probably take a practice test (similar to the tests in this book) during your class review.

Also, remember that any time you are using English Language Arts skills, you are "reviewing" for the test.

Is there anything I can do at home to prepare for the test?

Probably the most important thing you can do to improve your English Language Art skills is to read. Reading increases your vocabulary, improves your spelling skills, helps you understand different writing styles, and makes it easier for you to understand what the author is trying to say. The more different types of reading that you do, about different subjects, the better you will become as a reader, and the better you will be able to understand the variety of reading and listening passages on this test.

Working on the exercises in this book will also help you be familiar with the test and confident in your ability to do well.

Is there anything special I should do the night before the test?

You should do the things you would normally do the night before any test. Get your normal amount of rest—do not stay up late to review, and do not spend ANY time worrying about how you will do.

Just relax and be confident that you have prepared for the test, and you will do your best.

Reminder

Your experience taking the English Language Arts 3 and 4 Tests probably made you realize that the test was not as difficult as you imagined it might be. You will find the same thing to be true for the ELA 5 test, especially if you prepare yourself for it.

The following chapters and "extra" information at the end will be an excellent means for doing that preparation.

READING COMPREHENSION: MULTIPLE-CHOICE RESPONSES

This part of the test asks you to read short passages about a variety of subjects and answer multiple-choice questions about them.

Even though you have answered this type of question throughout your school career, you should find it helpful to review the types of questions that will be asked and the strategies to answer them.

The practice exercises are modeled after those that appeared on the *2006 New York State Grade 5 English Language Arts Test.*

IN THIS CHAPTER YOU WILL FIND

- explanations of the types of questions you will be asked;
- strategies and tips on how to answer these questions;
- practice passages and explanations of how to arrive at the correct answers.

TYPES OF QUESTIONS

Several different types of questions may be asked on this part of the test.

■ **FACT-BASED**

The answers to these questions can be found in the reading passage. You do not need to know anything about the subject of the passages.

■ **AUTHOR'S PURPOSE**

These questions are about what the author of the passage is trying to accomplish by writing the passage.

■ **THEME**

These questions ask you to figure out the message (also called MAIN IDEA, or point) of the passage.

■ **BEST TITLE**

These questions are similar to THEME questions, since most titles are based on what the passage is about.

■ **CAUSE and EFFECT**

These questions ask you to figure out how events relate to each other.

■ **SEQUENCE**

These questions ask you to put events in the order that they happened in the reading passage.

■ **CHARACTER-BASED**

These questions ask about a character in the passage. The answers may be fact-based or they may be about the character . . . possibly asking why the character did something or what the character is like.

■ PLOT-BASED

These questions are about events of the story. They may include sequence questions, cause and effect, compare and contrast, and others that are about what happens in the story.

■ VOCABULARY

These questions will ask you to select the correct meaning of words in the passage. Sometimes you will know them; sometimes you may have to figure out the best answer from clues in the passage.

TIPS

Read the questions carefully.

It is very important to understand what the question is asking and the type of answer it is looking for.

Look for key words that will help you locate the answer.

Different kinds of questions have different kinds of key words.

Read all the answers first.

Try to eliminate (get rid of) all the answers that seem to be WRONG. Then, pick the BEST answer from those that are left. Just because you find answers that are true, they are not necessarily correct.

Sometimes two answers are similar. Choose the one that is better.

Think of it as being "more correct" than the other. Only one choice can be the correct answer.

■ You can make INFERENCES based on facts in the reading AND facts that you know.

■ For FACT-BASED questions, base your answer only on the information in the passage.

■ For VOCABULARY questions, use context clues to help make the meaning clear. Ask yourself how the word fits into the sentence.

■ For VOCABULARY questions, see if the word you choose makes sense if you put it in the place of the word you are given.

KEY WORDS

■ For FACT-BASED questions, look for NAMES of people and places, DATES, and TITLES.

■ Some questions may ask which choice IS NOT correct. Be sure to look for words like *not* or *except.* These words are usually CAPITALIZED and/or in bold print.

■ Most SEQUENCE questions will deal with time order (chronological) or order of "doing." Look for words such as *first, next, then, before, after, last,* and *finally.* ALSO, look for dates.

■ Some SEQUENCE questions relate to order of importance. Look for words like *most, least, best, worst, first,* and *last.*

■ For CAUSE and EFFECT and COMPARE/CONTRAST questions, be sure to look for words that relate two or more things to each other.
  • Words such as *and, with, likewise,* and *also* tie things together and show similarity.
  • Words such as *but, however, instead,* and *despite* disconnect things and indicate an opposite sense or meaning.

READING COMPREHENSION: PRACTICE EXERCISES

Directions:

Read each passage carefully. Then answer the questions that follow. Choose the best answer for each question.

After you have completed the practice exercises, look at the next section to find the correct answers and explanations of the techniques used to arrive at the correct responses.

PRACTICE EXERCISE 1

Larry Doby: There's Nothing Wrong with Being Second

Many people know that Jackie Robinson was a pioneer. He was the first African American to play baseball in the modern major leagues. Robinson joined the National

League's Brooklyn Dodgers in 1947. Most people do not know who the second African American ballplayer was.

It was Larry Doby. He joined the Cleveland Indians of the American League just 11 weeks after Robinson's debut with the Dodgers.

He didn't start out in life hoping for a career in baseball. He once said that he grew up wanting to teach and coach in high school. But in 1942, while he was still in high school, he tried out for the Newark Eagles Negro League baseball team.

"They gave me a tryout, and I made the team," Doby said. "That's how I got involved in professional baseball."

When he joined the Cleveland Indians, he faced the same troubles that Robinson did. He had to work very hard to succeed, because of his race.

When he became manager of the Chicago White Sox in 1978, he was only the second African American to manage a major-league team. Because of his outstanding career, he was elected to the Baseball Hall of Fame in 1998.

1. Which of the following is most likely the author's purpose for writing this piece?

   A. to show which of the two players was better

   B. to pay tribute to Larry Doby

   C. to tell what a good player Larry Doby was

   D. to tell what a good player Jackie Robinson was

2. In the first sentence, the word *pioneer* most likely means

   A. an early settler of the Old West

   B. the first person to perform a historic task

   C. a person known for his athletic skill

   D. a person who became famous

3. Besides being the second African American player, he was also the second African American

   A. pitcher

   B. owner

   C. broadcaster

   D. manager

4. As used in the second paragraph, the word *debut* refers to Jackie Robinson's

   A. first game

   B. last game

   C. best game

   D. worst game

PRACTICE EXERCISE 2

Not as Smart as We Thought

In seventh grade, my friends Jim and Tony and I teamed up on a science project. It was during the time that space exploration was just beginning. We discovered that if you cut a drinking straw to slightly less than the width of your hand, it becomes a very effective missile launcher. Bits of notepaper rolled into the shape of a cone created perfect missiles. We practiced our marksmanship on the playground, on the way home, and in our basements. We became so good that we couldn't resist showing off a bit in school.

For a couple of days we launched our missiles in Mrs. C's English class. We were not very accurate because we had to be quick with our launches. On the other hand, we were thrilled to be getting away with being so sneaky.

Before you get the wrong idea, we were not bad kids. None of us had ever even received a detention. Also, we were three of the top students in seventh-grade English. On the third day of our missile launching experiment, Mrs. C called me into her room after lunch. She told me that she thought that some of the boys in Period 5 English might be shooting rolled up papers around her room. I wanted to ask why she thought it had to be boys, but I didn't.

She *knew* I wasn't involved, she said, and because the other boys respected me, I might be able to get them to stop. I assured her that I would do my best.

So, when the three of us got together after school, I told them the story. I was very smug because I had gotten away with it. I knew that she probably suspected them, though. She was using me as a way to get them to stop. I admit that I felt a little guilty, but I was still pleased that I was not a suspect.

With very odd looks on their faces, Jim and Tony said that Mrs. C had called each of them in, separately, and had the exact same conversation she had had with me.

No one else in the class had been shooting the paper missiles—no one else in the class had been called in. The three guilty rocketeers realized just what had happened. We discovered we weren't as smart as we thought. She had known all along. She had also given us credit for being good kids and trusted us to not make the same mistake again. And the next day when she acted surprised at finding a box of candy on her desk, she winked knowingly at us to seal the deal.

5. In the last paragraph it says, "The three guilty rocketeers realized just what had happened." What had happened?

   A. They had managed to fool the science teacher.

   B. They had managed to fool the English teacher.

   C. They had been outsmarted by their teacher.

   D. They received a good grade on the project.

6. The author's purpose in writing this story was most likely to

   A. show how smart the boys were in English and science

   B. show how sneaky the boys were in class

   C. show how a good teacher handles a problem

   D. show how to get away with mischief in school

7. According to the story, another good title might be

   A. "Teachers Are Always Right"

   B. "An Interesting Punishment"

   C. "Good Boys Gone Bad"

   D. "A Clever Solution"

8. What might be a reason that Mrs. C didn't punish the boys?

   A. she hadn't caught them doing it

   B. she wasn't sure they were guilty

   C. she liked their clever invention

   D. she knew her way would work better

PRACTICE EXERCISE 3

Getting There Was Not Easy

Shaquille Rashaun O'Neal was born on March 6, 1972. Today, he is better known as just "Shaq." At 7'1" and 315 pounds he is hard to miss. He is one of the most famous professional players in the world. He is also, occasionally, a rap singer and a movie actor. He is a college graduate and has earned a master's degree in business. He donates time and money to worthy causes.

Since his father was in the U.S. Army, Shaquille grew up as a "military brat," traveling to many places where his father was stationed. Partly because of his many moves, it was difficult for Shaquille to make friends. Also, because of his size (when he was 13, he stood 6' 5"), Shaquille was ignored by his peers in school. He felt that it was important for him to be popular, and he did many things to bring attention to himself.

In order to become popular he got involved in a lot of bad behavior. He thought that he could get the other kids to look up to him, not only for his height but because he was willing to do a lot of risky things. Unfortunately, the risky things were not examples of good behavior. It was definitely not the kind of behavior that his parents wanted for him. They wanted him to follow The Golden Rule: to treat others as he would like to be treated. As his show-off behavior got worse, his father decided it was time to turn Shaquille around.

Shaquille found himself constantly being punished for his bad behavior. His father, an army sergeant, was used to enforcing discipline and order among his soldiers, and that's exactly what he did with Shaquille. His father insisted that if he was going to play on the team, he needed to be a leader, not a follower—and he definitely could not behave badly.

Even though Shaquille was big, he was not a good athlete because he had no discipline. In the ninth grade he was cut from the basketball team. Once he started doing the right thing, leading by good examples instead of bad, Shaquille became a much better athlete and a better person. "I just had to practice, practice, and practice," he said. "I became a pretty good athlete after hard work."

He also became a better person.

9. According to the story, "to look up to someone" most likely means

   A. to understand him

   B. to know him

   C. to like him

   D. to dislike him

10. According to the story, Shaquille O'Neal's parents most likely wanted Shaq to become

A. a good basketball player

B. a good student

C. a good person

D. a good joker

11. In the second paragraph the word *peers* refers to

A. his fellow students

B. his teachers and administrators

C. his coaches and teachers

D. his parents and teachers

12. The author probably wrote this story to give advice to

A. basketball fans

B. basketball players

C. practical jokers

D. young people

PRACTICE EXERCISE 4

From Country Veterinarian to Famous Author

James Alfred Wight, also known as Alf Wight, was born in October 1916 in Sunderland, England. He grew up in Glasgow in Scotland. This is where he attended primary school and high school.

He dreamed of becoming a veterinarian, called a veterinary surgeon in Britain. In 1939 he "qualified" by graduating from Glasgow Veterinary College. Then, he moved to the Yorkshire area of England. In the town of Thirsk, he was hired by a veterinarian named Donald Sinclair.

James had wanted to work with small animals—dogs and cats. However, Yorkshire was farm country. He worked mostly with large animals like horses and cows and a lot with pigs and sheep. He worked many hours in the cold and rain delivering thousands of baby animals.

Slowly, people began to realize that their smaller animals needed care too. Alf Wight became an expert with dogs, cats, and other small animals as well.

Alf wanted to write about his adventures as a vet. Because his work took up so much of his time, he didn't get to write about them until he was 50.

He wasn't sure that people would think his writing would be good. He chose the pen name "James Herriot" (from the name of a popular Scottish soccer player, Jimmy Herriot) to disguise himself.

He wrote a series of books, beginning with *If Only They Could Talk*. By the time he died, in 1995, he had written 11 books about his adventures with animals. They were also made into two movies and a British television series called *All Creatures Great and Small*. James Herriot had become a name known all over the world.

13. A "pen name" is a name chosen to be used by

   A. a veterinarian

   B. a farmer

   C. an author

   D. an animal

14. What did James Herriot NOT do?

   A. grow up in Scotland

   B. become an author

   C. work in a large city

   D. work with horses

15. As used in this story, the term *delivering* refers to:

    A. bringing mail to people on farms

    B. helping with the birth of animals

    C. doing good deeds in school

    D. working for a veterinarian

16. Which did Mr. Herriot do last?

    A. work as a veterinarian for dogs

    B. write about his work with animals

    C. attend college in Glasgow

    D. dream about being a veterinarian

PRACTICE EXERCISE 5

The Main Street Elementary School Fourth-Grade Girls Free-Throw Shooting Contest Overtime Sudden Victory Shootout

Of the 16 entrants, two remained.
Now trying to break the tie,
Rebecca bounced the ball
between her nine-year-old toes,
caught it,

squeezed it in her hands,
squinted at her target
drew the ball back,
and FLUNG it at the far off hoop.

It wobbled through the gymnasium's silent air,
CLANGED onto the rim,
BOUNCED, once, twice,
on the orange iron,
BALANCED for a second,
deciding which way to go,
then sort of LEANED over the side
and fell OFF the rim
on the outside,
and DROPPED to the floor.

The crowd sighed politely,
a couple of groans,
then cheers for the winner.

What I saw was
Rebecca
TROT to the line,
dribble the ball back and forth from hand to hand,
SPIN IT expertly in her palm,
DIP at the knees and release
it from her fingertips
with a practiced FLICK of the wrist
that ARCHES it expertly toward the hoop.

It HANGS in the air for the merest moment before
SNAPPING through the net with the
SWISH of perfection.

So when she walked up to me and said,
"That was fun, Grampa,"
I knew what I had seen was real,
and we both had won.

17. This is a narrative poem because it

    A. uses poetic devices

    B. tells a story

    C. creates a mood

    D. turns out happy

18. The words *clang* and *swish* describe

    A. calls made by the referee

    B. noises made by the crowd

    C. sounds made by the scoreboard

    D. sounds made by the basketball

19. The phrase *gymnasium's silent air* is an example of which poetic device?

    A. simile

    B. hyperbole

    C. metaphor

    D. foreshadowing

20. The poet creates a mood in the poem that is best described as

    A. happy

    B. sad

    C. relaxed

    D. tense

21. The poet most likely capitalized some of the words

    A. because they are supposed to be

    B. because he was careless

    C. to make them seem important

    D. to make them interesting

On the actual test, a short response question will appear directly after the multiple-choice questions. It will be based on a reading passage. Refer to chapter 3 for review.

IMPORTANT INFORMATION

Before going on to the next chapter, you should review the questions that you got wrong and be sure that you understand WHY they were wrong and HOW to find the correct answer.

Then, you should review your correct answers to be sure you understand WHY and HOW they were correct. If you got them right by making educated guesses based on strategies, that is good and will help you do well on this type of question.

If you got them right because you made wild guesses and were lucky to get them right, review them just as you would review the questions you missed, because you can't count on making lucky guesses on the actual test.

After you are satisfied that you know how to do this type of question, move on to the next chapter.

LISTENING COMPREHENSION

STRATEGIES AND TIPS

In this part of the test, you will have a passage read to you twice. You will be able to take notes on the passage and then you will answer questions just like in the reading comprehension section. The only difference is that instead of having the actual reading passage to go back to for help with your answers, you will have your notes and your memory to help.

The most important advice for this section is to pay attention, listen carefully and take good notes.

In This Chapter You Will Find

- strategies and tips on how to answer these questions;
- tips on taking notes;
- practice passages and explanations of how to arrive at the correct answers.

LISTEN TO THE PASSAGES CAREFULLY

By listening carefully, you will have a clear idea of what the passage is "about." Careful listening will also help you remember important things in the passage, and make it easier for you to take notes and go back and use them to find the answers to the questions that follow the reading of the passage.

- Always try to determine the MAIN IDEA. That will help you understand the questions you are asked.
- Once you have the main idea, **listen for details that support (give information about) it.** These details are often the answers to FACT-BASED questions. They are also often used as part of the question, so if you have listened carefully, and taken good notes, you will be able to remember them.
- **Read the questions carefully.** It is very important to understand what the question is asking and the type of answer it is looking for.
- Once you understand what the question is asking, **look for KEY WORDS in your notes that will help you locate the answer.** Different kinds of questions have different kinds of key words.
- **Read all the answers first.** Try to eliminate (get rid of) all the answers that seem to be WRONG. Then, pick the BEST answer from those that are left. Just because you find answers that are true, they are not necessarily correct.
- Sometimes two answers are similar. **Choose the one that is best.** Think of it as being "more correct" than the other; only one choice can be the correct answer.
- You can make **inferences** based on facts in the reading AND facts that you know.
- For FACT-BASED questions, base your answer only on the information in the passage.
- For VOCABULARY questions, **use context clues** to help make the meaning clear. Ask yourself how the word fits into the sentence.
- For VOCABULARY questions, see if the word you choose makes sense if you put it in the place of the word you are given.

TIPS FOR TAKING NOTES

- The passage(s) will be read to you TWICE. The directions say that you are not to take notes during the first reading and to just listen carefully. This will help you understand the passage as a whole, get the main idea in mind, and listen for key words that will be important when you take notes during the second reading.

■ The reason it is suggested that you only listen the first time through is that you might find yourself concentrating so hard on taking good notes that you neglect to completely pay attention to the reading. It is very difficult to concentrate on two things at once.

■ You have a lot of experience taking notes in class, and the practice exercises and practice tests in this book will help you get comfortable with the way this will work on the test.

KEY WORDS

■ **NAMES** of **PEOPLE, PLACES, DATES,** and **TITLES** will often be answers for **FACT-BASED** questions.

■ Some questions may ask which choice **IS NOT** correct. Be sure to listen for words like *not* or *except* when you are taking notes. These words are usually **CAPITALIZED** and/or in bold print.

■ Most **SEQUENCE** questions will deal with time order (chronological) or order of "doing." Listen for words such as *first, next, then, before, after, last,* and *finally.* ALSO, listen for times and dates.

■ Some **SEQUENCE** questions relate to order of importance. Listen for words like *most, least, best, worst, first,* and *last.*

■ For CAUSE and EFFECT and COMPARE/CONTRAST questions, be sure to look for words in your notes that relate two or more things to each other.

■ Words such as *and, with, likewise,* and *also* tie things together and show similar ideas.

■ Words such as *but, however, instead,* and *despite* disconnect things and show an opposite sense or meaning.

NOTE: Following are some practice listening passages and exercises. For practice purposes, these should be read aloud by an accomplished reader. A teacher or other adult would be best. The reader should practice the passage beforehand and should read clearly at a comfortable pace. The passage *should not* be read as dictation, and should be read from start to finish. Then, after a short pause, it should be read a second time. After the second reading, the student should answer the question for that passage only.

On the actual test, and on the practice tests found later in this book, the appropriate time limits should be enforced. For the purposes of these shorter practice exercises, no time limit is necessary. It is more important to become familiar with the process at this point.

STOP! Please have a teacher or parent read the following listening passages.

LISTENING PRACTICE EXERCISE

PASSAGE 1

One-Room Schoolhouse

From Bland County History Archives–Rocky Gap, VA

One-room schoolhouses were the backbone of education in Bland County (Virginia). The schools gave the area children a first through seventh grade education. They were taught reading, writing, and arithmetic in the lower grades. Science, geography, and literature were taught in the upper grades.

The schools were all within walking distance of the students who attended them. There was no public transportation. They had to either walk or ride a horse to school.

Liberty, a school on Route 42, is just one example. The building was one room with weather-boarded walls. The blackboards were real slate. Located in the center of the room was a potbellied stove. This provided heat during the winter months. Parents always furnished the wood and the older boys were let out of class to split it for the next day. In the corner of the school was a table with water and a dipper, which provided water for the students throughout the day and at lunch.

There was no cafeteria. They brought lunch from home. Many of the lunches were biscuits with beef or homemade jelly, fruit, and a piece of cake or pie was very common. During lunch they had time to play games such as Annie over, baseball, and many others.

Holidays were always celebrated in these small schools. Christmas was the most remembered. The room was decorated with popcorn wreaths and paper cutouts made by the children. The children always had a Christmas program for their parents. There was never a fee and all the parents came.

These schools were run by one person, the teacher. Ora Gray Stowers taught at the Liberty school. She said there was "never any rudeness or discourtesy to small children in school." She said that she did have to use a little switch or paddle when a ruckus started, but according to her it wasn't very often. She said the worst punishment was standing in the corner in front of everyone because she thought this embarrassed them.

Jessie Hart Finley who was a student at Silver Creek said that she could recall some of the boys were as old as 18 and still in the seventh grade. This was because they couldn't go anywhere else to get an education. The closest school that offered any higher classes was five miles away. This was Hollybrook. Hollybrook taught up to the tenth grade. But since there was no transportation offered to the boys they had no way of getting there unless they walked, so they just kept coming to Silver Creek.

These one room schools have been long forgotten, but they served Bland County for many years. They taught the children everything they needed to know from reading, writing, and arithmetic to discipline and manners.

LISTENING PRACTICE—PASSAGE 1 QUESTIONS

Choose the best answer for each question.

1. One-room schoolhouses were the backbone of education in Bland County. As it is used in this passage, the word *backbone* most nearly means

   A. the main part

   B. one of several kinds

   C. a new type of building

   D. a problem

2. According to the passage, the word *ruckus* most nearly means

   A. snowstorm

   B. illness

   C. disturbance

   D. test

3. Based on the information in the passage, Liberty school was most likely located

   A. in a city

   B. in the country

   C. in the desert

   D. in a resort

4. According to the passage, which subject was not taught until the upper grades?

A. reading

B. writing

C. arithmetic

D. science

5. A teacher in a one-room school would have to know how to

A. teach many subjects

B. chop firewood

C. drive a school bus

D. coach baseball

LISTENING PRACTICE EXERCISE

PASSAGE 2

Down the Real Yellow Brick Road

If you are ever in the small town of Chittenango, New York in early June, you might find yourself amazed at what you see. You might swear that you are driving through a town full of characters from the Wizard of Oz. You might even think you *are* in Oz. You would see Dorothy and the Cowardly Lion and the Tin Woodman and the Scarecrow. There would be Toto and witches and Munchkins.

You will see them during the annual Oz Fest. It is called the Oz Fest because you are in the hometown of L. Frank Baum who wrote *The Wizard of Oz*. It is one of the most famous children's stories ever written.

Lyman Frank Baum was born in Chittenango in 1857. He started writing when he was young. His father gave him a printing press and he and his brother Henry started a newspaper. He also had an interest in acting that lasted his whole life.

He and his family lived in many places around the country. He worked for and owned several newspapers. He also traveled a lot as a salesman and theater manager. While he traveled, he made up stories to entertain his children. He published several books. That allowed him to stop traveling and spend his time writing more books.

In 1900, he published *The Wonderful Wizard of Oz*. This is the book that made him famous. It was so popular that it was the best-selling children's book for two years. He wrote thirteen more books about the people of the Land of Oz.

He continued to write children's books under several different names. He also wrote for adult readers. Eventually, he wrote more than a hundred books. He also wrote plays, magazine articles, and short stories. He became a very successful writer and publisher.

He and his family moved to Hollywood, California. He turned his Oz stories into plays and in 1914, into movies. The movies were not successful because they were children's stories and children didn't go to movies much then.

He continued to be a popular and successful writer until his death in 1919. But that is not the end of his story.

His dream of having *The Wonderful Wizard of Oz* become a successful movie eventually would come true. In 1939, the movie we know as simply *The Wizard of Oz* was released. It has become one of the most popular movies of all time. Children *and* adults love it even today, nearly seventy years later.

So, if you are ever in Chittenango in early June, don't think you are dreaming. Just enjoy your trip down the yellow brick road with Dorothy and all her friends.

LISTENING PRACTICE—PASSAGE 2 QUESTIONS

Choose the best answer for each question.

6. The Oz Fest is most likely in Chittenango because
   A. it is Dorothy's hometown
   B. it is L. Frank Baum's hometown
   C. *The Wizard of Oz* was filmed there
   D. it used to be called "Oz"

7. L. Frank Baum's books started out as
   A. stories he told his friends
   B. the diary he wrote in the army
   C. stories to entertain his children
   D. a movie he saw in Hollywood

8. How many *Oz* books were published AFTER *The Wonderful Wizard of Oz*?
   A. 10
   B. 11
   C. 12
   D. 13

9. L. Frank Baum was probably able to write so many children's books because he

   A. had a good typewriter

   B. believed in witches

   C. had a good imagination

   D. had plenty of spare time

10. According to the passage, the 1939 version of *The Wizard of Oz* was MOST LIKELY popular because

   A. it was in color

   B. it had good actors

   C. children loved it

   D. the effects were realistic

LISTENING PRACTICE EXERCISE

PASSAGE 3

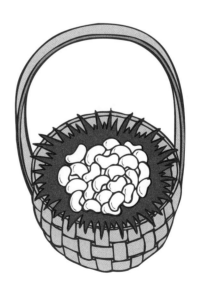

A Very Old Candy

No one is exactly sure about the history of jelly beans, but we know they are a very old candy.

Many candy experts think the inside of jelly beans are related to a soft Mid-Eastern candy known as Turkish Delight. These candies are probably more than a thousand years old.

The coating probably comes from France. It was originally part of making a candy called Jordan Almonds. It was first used in the 17th century. The process is almost the same now, except it is done by machines today.

The French began coating almonds with sugar and syrup in bowls. Today, large automatic pans do the work. Eventually the two processes were combined.

In America, jelly beans became a very popular "penny candy." They were sold in general stores, where they were stored in glass jars. People could choose the colors they wanted. The beans would be weighed and put in paper bags to take home.

In the 1930s, jelly beans became part of our Easter traditions. Candy historians think that because of their egg-like shape they were associated with the Easter Bunny. He is believed to deliver eggs as a symbol of new life during the spring season, and jelly beans became part of the tradition.

It takes a week or more to make a jelly bean. Jelly bean makers start with the center of the jelly bean. Sugar, corn syrup and other ingredients are cooked in large vats. The mixture is put into molds to harden. Then a shiny glaze is sprayed on the candy. The beans harden for three to four days and then they are ready to eat.

Since about 1976, there have been two types of jelly beans. Gourmet and traditional jelly beans have slightly different recipes. Gourmet jelly beans are usually softer and smaller than traditional jelly beans. In addition, gourmet jelly beans have flavoring in both the shell and the center. The traditional beans usually have only a flavored shell.

Jelly beans became very popular when Ronald Reagan was president of the United States. He loved jelly beans, and always had a jar of them on his desk.

LISTENING PRACTICE—PASSAGE 3 QUESTIONS

Choose the best answer for each question.

11. As used in the passage, the word *glaze* most nearly means a

   A. coating for the outside

   B. flavoring for the center

   C. hardener for the shell

   D. softener for the jelly

12. Since 1976, there have been

   A. two types of jelly beans

   B. two different flavors

   C. two new ingredients

   D. two different prices

13. Jelly beans became associated with Easter mostly because of their

   A. size

   B. cost

   C. taste

   D. shape

14. According to the passage, one way that gourmet jelly beans are different from traditional jelly beans is that they are

    A. cheaper

    B. smaller

    C. better

    D. cleaner

15. According to the passage, the most likely reason that jelly beans are still popular today is that they are

    A. long lasting

    B. easy to carry

    C. part of Easter

    D. good tasting

16. Another good title for this passage would be

    A. "An Easter Tradition"

    B. "My Favorite Candy"

    C. "A History of Jelly Beans"

    D. "Candy Making in France"

LISTENING PRACTICE EXERCISE

PASSAGE 4

The Strange Career of Moe Berg

There is a saying that "truth is often stranger than fiction." The life of a man named Moe Berg is proof of that saying.

Morris Berg was born in 1902 in Newark, New Jersey. He went by the nickname "Moe" for most of his life. After graduating number one in his high school class, he went to Princeton University. That was quite an accomplishment for a poor Jewish boy in the 1920s.

Berg was an excellent student at Princeton. He studied Latin, Greek, French, Spanish, Italian, German, and Sanskrit. Eventually he was able to read and write 12 languages. Not only did he graduate at the top of his class, he also became the star shortstop of the college baseball team.

In order to pay to continue his education, he accepted a contract to play professional baseball. He played shortstop for the Brooklyn Dodgers and later, the Chicago White Sox. At the same time, he attended Columbia Law School and finished second in his class.

The White Sox changed his position to catcher. That position took advantage of his strong arm and intelligence. In 1929 he batted .287 and received votes for Most Valuable Player. In 1930 he seriously injured his knee, ending his career as a full-time player. He played as a substitute for three more teams until he retired in 1939. He had played 15 years in the major leagues.

So far, his story is only a little bit unusual. It was soon to become almost unbelievable.

In 1934, Moe toured Japan with a group of major league all-stars that included Babe Ruth and Lou Gehrig. Because of his great language skills, he was invited to lecture at a Japanese University. He gave his speech in Japanese.

Before the trip, the U.S. government had recruited Berg as a spy. While visiting an American at a Tokyo hospital, he sneaked onto the roof and took photos of the city. Pilots later used the photos during bombing raids in World War II.

Berg volunteered to serve when America entered the war in 1941. He began work for the Office of Strategic Services, which later became the Central Intelligence Agency. In a few weeks of studying, the brilliant Berg taught himself a great deal about nuclear physics. Even though it was dangerous, he spent parts of 1944 and 1945 in Germany. He helped set up the capture of several important German atomic scientists by U.S. troops before the Russians could get them.

He traveled through Europe and discovered that a factory in Norway was producing atomic bomb parts for the Nazis. Allied planes bombed the factory. He even parachuted into Yugoslavia in search of important information.

After the war, Moe Berg was offered the Medal of Merit. The medal was the highest award that could be given to a civilian. He declined it because he was not looking for fame.

There are many stories about how he spent the rest of his life. Most of them are about the mysterious way he lived. No one really knows much about that time, but Casey Stengel called him "the strangest man that ever played baseball."

LISTENING PRACTICE - PASSAGE 4 QUESTIONS

Choose the best answer for each question.

17. According to the story, we know that Moe Berg spoke
- **A.** Dutch
- **B.** Japanese
- **C.** Russian
- **D.** Swedish

18. According to the story, we know that Moe traveled to each country EXCEPT

  A. Yugoslavia

  B. Germany

  C. Brazil

  D. Japan

19. As it is used in the story, the word *brilliant* most closely means

  A. athletic

  B. intelligent

  C. modest

  D. generous

20. According to the story, Moe Berg definitely played for what major-league teams?

  A. Giants and Yankees

  B. Dodgers and Yankees

  C. Yankees and White Sox

  D. Dodgers and White Sox

21. Another good title for this story would be

  A. "A Brave and Talented Man"

  B. "How to Learn a Foreign Language"

  C. "Babe Ruth's Friend"

  D. "A Dangerous Job"

On the actual test, a short response question will appear directly after the multiple-choice questions. It will be based on a reading passage. Refer to chapter 3 for review.

IMPORTANT INFORMATION

Before going on to the next chapter, you should review the questions that you got wrong and be sure that you understand **WHY** they were wrong and **HOW** to find the correct answer.

Then, you should review your correct answers to be sure you understand **WHY** and **HOW** they were correct. If you got them right by making educated guesses based on strategies, that is good and will help you do well on this type of question.

If you got them right because you made wild guesses and were lucky to get them right, review them just as you would review the questions you missed, because you can't count on making lucky guesses on the actual test.

After you are satisfied that you know how to do this type of question, move on to the next chapter.

SHORT RESPONSE

In both the READING and LISTENING sections, which you have already practiced, you will be asked to respond to questions with a short response. This chapter will give you some tips and practice on that kind of question.

Unless the question asks you to LIST your answers, you should write in complete sentences to get full credit.

This type of question is NOT an essay question, but more of a fill in the blank.

You will see from the amount of space given for your answer that a long answer is NOT expected.

TIPS

- Read the question carefully so that you understand exactly what kind of answer you should give.
- Since most questions require you to use details (information) from the passage, you need to understand what type of information to use.
- Some questions will tell you to use DETAILS from the passage to support your answer. Usually DETAILS means more than one but it does not have to be more than two. If the question asks for a certain number of DETAILS, give exactly that many.
- Some questions will tell you to use INFORMATION from the passage to support your answer. This is a

different way of asking for details. Give enough to support (back up) your answer.

▪ Most short response questions may be answered by remembering the WWWWWH (*Who, What, Why, Where, When, and How*) guideline that you may already know. These are the words that begin, or are contained in, **most** questions.

▪ Be sure that the details (information) that you use are related to (are about) what the question asks. By carefully reading the question to understand what it is about, you will be able to respond to it by giving details that support your answer.

WWWWWH CHART

If you think about the key question word (WWWWWH), it will help you find the kind of detail or details that will best answer that question.

Key Word	Kinds of Details to Use
Who	People, either named or described. They do things or have things done to them. *Who* can also be animals or other characters.
What	Things or actions
Why	Reasons for something. The cause of something.
When	Time, dates, seasons, time periods, and historic periods
Where	Places, areas, locations, and scene settings
How	The way something is done

SHORT RESPONSE: PRACTICE EXERCISES

Read the passages, and then answer the questions. Be sure to read each question carefully so that you understand exactly what it is asking.

PASSAGE 1

Larry Doby: There's Nothing Wrong with Being Second

Many people know that Jackie Robinson was a pioneer. He was the first African American to play baseball in the modern major leagues. Robinson joined the National League's Brooklyn Dodgers in 1947. Most people do not know who the second African American ballplayer was.

It was Larry Doby. He joined the Cleveland Indians of the American League just 11 weeks after Robinson's debut with the Dodgers.

He didn't start out in life hoping for a career in baseball. He once said that he grew up wanting to teach and coach in high school. But in 1942, while he was still in high school, he tried out for the Newark Eagles Negro League baseball team.

"They gave me a tryout, and I made the team," Doby said. "That's how I got involved in professional baseball."

When he joined the Cleveland Indians, he faced the same troubles that Robinson did. He had to work very hard to succeed, because of his race.

When he became manager of the Chicago White Sox in 1978, he was only the second African American to manage a major-league team. Because of his outstanding career he was elected to the Baseball Hall of Fame in 1998.

QUESTION 1: Use details from the passage to show why the title is a good one.

_____

_____

_____

_____

PASSAGE 2

The Main Street Elementary School Fourth-Grade Girls Free-Throw Shooting Contest Overtime Sudden Victory Shootout

Of the 16 entrants, two remained.
Now trying to break the tie,
Rebecca bounced the ball
between her nine-year-old toes,
caught it,
squeezed it in her hands,
squinted at her target
drew the ball back,
and FLUNG it at the far off hoop.

It wobbled through the gymnasium's silent air,
CLANGED onto the rim,
BOUNCED, once, twice,
on the orange iron,
BALANCED for a second,
deciding which way to go,
then sort of LEANED over the side
and fell OFF the rim
on the outside,
and DROPPED to the floor.

The crowd sighed politely,
a couple of groans,
then cheers for the winner.

What I saw was
Rebecca TROT to the line,
dribble the ball back and forth from hand to hand,
SPIN IT expertly in her palm,
DIP at the knees and release
it from her fingertips
with a practiced FLICK of the wrist
that ARCHES it expertly toward the hoop.

It HANGS in the air for the merest moment before
SNAPPING through the net with the
SWISH of perfection.

So when she walked up to me and said,
"That was fun, Grampa,"
I knew what I had seen was real,
and we both had won.

QUESTION 2: Use details from the poem to show why
the poet says they "both had won."

_____

_____

_____

PASSAGE 3

From Country Veterinarian to Famous Author

James Alfred Wight, also known as Alf Wight, was born
in October 1916 in Sunderland, England. He grew up in

Glasgow in Scotland. This is where he attended primary school and high school.

He dreamed of becoming a veterinarian, called a veterinary surgeon in Britain. In 1939 he "qualified" by graduating from Glasgow Veterinary College. Then, he moved to the Yorkshire area of England. In the town of Thirsk, he was hired by a veterinarian named Donald Sinclair.

James had wanted to work with small animals—dogs and cats. However, Yorkshire was farm country. He worked mostly with large animals like horses and cows and a lot with pigs and sheep. He worked many hours in the cold and rain delivering thousands of baby animals.

Slowly, people began to realize that their smaller animals needed care too. Alf Wight became an expert with dogs, cats, and other small animals as well.

Alf wanted to write about his adventures as a vet. Because his work took up so much of his time, he didn't get to write about them until he was 50.

He wasn't sure that people would think his writing would be good. He chose the pen name "James Herriot" (from the name of a popular Scottish soccer player, Jimmy Herriot) to disguise himself.

He wrote a series of books, beginning with *If Only They Could Talk*. By the time he died, in 1995, he had written 11 books about his adventures with animals. They were also made into two movies and a British television series called *All Creatures Great and Small*. James Herriot had become a name known all over the world.

QUESTION 3: Using information from the passage, explain three things that Alf Wight did that helped him become the famous writer, James Herriot.

_____

_____

_____

PASSAGE 4

A Very Old Candy

No one is exactly sure about the history of jelly beans, but we know they are a very old candy.

Many candy experts think the inside of jelly beans are related to a soft Mid-Eastern candy known as Turkish Delight. These candies are probably more than a thousand years old.

The coating probably comes from France. It was originally part of making a candy called Jordan Almonds. It was first used in the 17th century. The process is almost the same now, except it is done by machines today.

The French began coating almonds with sugar and syrup in bowls. Today, large automatic pans do the work. Eventually the two processes were combined.

In America, jelly beans became a very popular "penny candy." They were sold in general stores, where they were stored in glass jars. People could choose the colors they wanted. The beans would be weighed and put in paper bags to take home.

In the 1930s, jelly beans became part of our Easter traditions. Candy historians think that because of their egg-like shape they were associated with the Easter Bunny. He is believed to deliver eggs as a symbol of new life during the spring season, and jelly beans became part of the tradition.

It takes a week or more to make a jelly bean. Jelly bean makers start with the center of the jelly bean. Sugar, corn syrup, and other ingredients are cooked in large vats. The mixture is put into molds to harden. Then a shiny glaze is added. The beans harden for three to four days and then they are ready to eat.

Since about 1976, there have been two types of jelly beans. Gourmet and traditional jelly beans have slightly different recipes. Gourmet jelly beans are usually softer and smaller than traditional jelly beans. In addition, gourmet jelly beans have flavoring in both the shell and the center. The traditional beans usually have only a flavored shell.

Jelly beans became really popular when Ronald Reagan was president of the United States. He loved jelly beans, and always had a jar of them on his desk.

QUESTION 4: Using details from the passage, compare the old and new ways of making jelly beans.

_____

_____

_____

PASSAGE 5

Down the Real Yellow Brick Road

If you are ever in the small town of Chittenango, New York in early June, you might find yourself amazed at what you see. You might swear that you are driving through a town full of characters from the Wizard of Oz. You might even think you *are* in Oz. You would see Dorothy and the Cowardly Lion and the Tin Woodman and the Scarecrow. There would be Toto and witches and Munchkins.

You will see them during the annual Oz Fest. It is called the Oz Fest because you are in the hometown of L. Frank Baum who wrote *The Wizard of Oz*. It is one of the most famous children's stories ever written.

Lyman Frank Baum was born in Chittenango in 1857. He started writing when he was young. His father gave him a printing press and he and his brother Henry started a newspaper. He also had an interest in acting that lasted his whole life.

He and his family lived in many places around the country. He worked for and owned several newspapers. He also traveled a lot as a salesman and theater manager. While he traveled, he made up stories to entertain his children. He published several books. That allowed him to stop traveling and spend his time writing more books.

In 1900, he published *The Wonderful Wizard of Oz*. This is the book that made him famous. It was so popular that it was the best-selling children's book for two years. He wrote thirteen more books about the people of the Land of Oz.

He continued to write children's books under several different names. He also wrote for adult readers. Eventually, he wrote more than a hundred books. He also wrote plays, magazine articles, and short stories. He became a very successful writer and publisher.

He and his family moved to Hollywood, California. He turned his Oz stories into plays and in 1914, into movies. The movies were not successful because they were children's stories and children didn't go to movies much then.

He continued to be a popular and successful writer until his death in 1919. But that is not the end of his story.

His dream of having *The Wonderful Wizard of Oz* become a successful movie eventually would come true. In 1939, the movie we know as simply *The Wizard of Oz* was released. It has become one of the most popular movies of all time. Children *and* adults love it even today, nearly seventy years later.

So, if you are ever in Chittenango in early June, don't think you are dreaming. Just enjoy your trip down the yellow brick road with Dorothy and all her friends.

QUESTION 5: Using details from the passage, tell how L. Frank Baum's real life made the Oz Fest possible.

_____

_____

_____

_____

SCORING THE SHORT RESPONSE QUESTIONS

Courtesy of the New York State Department of Education.

SCORING RUBRIC: 2-POINT RUBRIC FOR SHORT RESPONSE QUESTIONS

2 points: The response is accurate and complete, and it fulfills all the requirements of the task. Necessary support and/or examples are included, and the information given is clearly text-based. Any extensions beyond the text are relevant to the task.

1 point: The response includes some correct information, but may be too general or overly specific. Some of the support and/or examples may be incomplete or omitted.

0 points: The response is inaccurate, confused, and/or irrelevant, or the student failed to respond to the task.

EDITING

An editor is someone who finds and fixes mistakes in writing pieces. In this question you will be doing just that. In the EDITING question, you will be asked to find and correct mistakes in a short piece of writing.

This is the same kind of question that is on the New York State ELA 3 Test. If you were not in New York for this test, it may *seem* new to you, but it is just doing the kind of work you do whenever you create a writing piece.

You are used to EDITING your own written work as well as helping your fellow students edit theirs when you have writing conferences. This is just like the way your teachers help you fix your writing in class. This question really is just about finding mistakes and fixing them.

Four important things to remember:

- There will be NO SPELLING ERRORS.
- There MAY be more than one way to correct some of the errors.
- You do not have to explain your answers. Just cross out what is wrong and NEATLY write in what is correct.
- If you are just removing something that doesn't belong, all you have to do is cross it out.

PUNCTUATION RULES *by Kimberly Steele*

For review and practice on the editing passage

Here are some basic rules that you have learned. You can review these before you do the practice exercises. These rules are about the kind of mistakes that might be in this section of the test.

NOTE: This is a very comprehensive list. Teachers/parents might wish to consult the New York State Core Curriculum (Appendix 3) to focus on certain areas. Asterisks (*) indicate more common errors to be found in the editing passages.

*PERIOD

1. Use a period at the end of a sentence.

    EXAMPLE: I enjoyed the movie.

2. Use a period after an initial.

    EXAMPLE: M. E. Kerr is a wonderful author.

3. Use a period after an abbreviation.

    EXAMPLE: We welcomed Mrs. Simmons to our
    team.

4. Use a period as a decimal point.

    EXAMPLE: The workers received a 2.1 percent
    raise.

5. Use a period to separate dollars and cents.

    EXAMPLE: The book cost $4.95.

6. Use a period after each number in a list printed vertically.

    EXAMPLE: For the example, look at the items on
    this page. They are in that form.

EXCLAMATION POINT

Use an exclamation point at the end of a sentence, phrase, or word to indicate strong emotion. (Never use more than one exclamation point.)

> EXAMPLE: Wow! I never thought Mom would let us go to the concert!

> Unacceptable: Wow!! I never thought Mom would let us go to the concert!!!!!!

QUESTION MARK

7. Use a question mark at the end of a question.

   > EXAMPLE: Did Steven go with you?

8. Use a question mark at the end of a declarative statement when you want to convey disbelief.

   > EXAMPLE: She's our new teacher?

9. Use a question mark with parentheses to indicate that you are not sure of a spelling or other fact.

   > EXAMPLE: I have to visit an orthopedic (?) doctor next week.

*COMMA

10. Use a comma after each item in a series of at least three items. (It has become acceptable to omit the comma before the conjunction in a series. However, it is important to remain consistent.)

    > EXAMPLE: I still need to take a test, write an essay, and check out a book.

    > EXAMPLE: I dislike spinach, broccoli, and cauliflower.

Acceptable: I dislike spinach, broccoli and cauliflower.

11. Use commas after the street address and city in an address. (Do not use a comma after the state.)

EXAMPLE: The address is 1234 Apple Street, Midtown, Kansas 98765.

12. Use a comma after the day and the year in a date. No comma is used if only the month and year are given.

EXAMPLE: Connie's birthday is February 20, 1965.

EXAMPLE: Connie was born in February 1965.

13. Use a comma to clarify large numbers. Counting from right to left, a comma is needed after every three digits. This rule does not apply to years, where no commas are used at all.

EXAMPLE: In 1998 the population of Claremont was 23,899.

14. Use a comma to separate two or more adjectives that equally modify the same noun. (If you aren't sure whether or not to use a comma to separate the adjectives, say the sentence with the word *and* in place of the comma. If it makes sense, then use the comma.)

EXAMPLE: Jill was having problems with the unruly, disruptive children.

15. Use a comma after a dependent clause that begins a sentence.

EXAMPLE: If Mr. Wilson complains, we'll invite him for a snack.

16. Use a comma before the conjunction in a compound sentence. However, if the two independent clauses are very short, you do not need the comma.

EXAMPLE: We had a lot of fun, so I'll have another party soon.

EXAMPLE: She spoke and I took notes.

17. When quoting, use a comma before the quotation.

EXAMPLE: Ariel said, "I knew you would win the contest."

18. Use a comma after a mild interjection, such as *oh* or *well*.

EXAMPLE: Oh, the test was not that difficult.

19. Use a comma after a noun of direct address.

EXAMPLE: Kodi, didn't I ask you to clean your room?

20. Use a comma after the greeting in a personal letter.

EXAMPLE: Dear Aunt Sheila,

21. Use a comma after the closing of a letter.

EXAMPLE: Sincerely,

22. Use a comma to indicate where a pause is necessary in order to avoid confusion. (Sometimes rewriting the sentence is a better choice.)

EXAMPLE: After Kelly, Jennifer gets a turn.

EXAMPLE: Maria came in, in quite a hurry.

23. Use a comma to set off the abbreviation *etc.*

EXAMPLE: I went to the store to get napkins, plates, cups, forks, etc.

24. Use a comma between a person's name and title.

EXAMPLE:

Anthony LaRussa, Attorney-at-Law

Hector Lopez, President

Barbara O'Neil Chrisley, CEO

SEMICOLON

25. Use a semicolon to join two independent clauses. (This eliminates the need for a comma and a conjunction.)

EXAMPLE: Casey read a book; then he did a book report.

26. Use a semicolon to separate items in a series when those items contain punctuation such as a comma.

EXAMPLE: We went on field trips to Topeka, Kansas; Freedom, Oklahoma; and Amarillo, Texas.

COLON

27. Use a colon between numerals indicating hours and minutes.

EXAMPLE: School starts at 8:05 A.M.

28. Use a colon to introduce a list that appears after an independent clause. (Introductory words such as *following* go somewhere before the colon to help introduce the list.)

EXAMPLE: You need the following items for class: pencil, pens, paper, ruler, and glue.

29. When mentioning a volume number and page number, use a colon between the two items.

> EXAMPLE: You will find information about Mexico in *Grolier Encyclopedia* 17:245.

30. Use a colon after the greeting of a business letter.

> EXAMPLE: Dear Sir:

31. Use a colon between the title and subtitle of a book.

> EXAMPLE: *Reading Strategies That Work: Teaching Your Students to Become Better Readers* is an excellent resource.

32. Use a colon between the chapter and verse numbers for parts of the Bible.

> EXAMPLE: Please read Genesis 1:3.

*APOSTROPHE

33. Use an apostrophe in a contraction to show where letters have been omitted, or left out.

> EXAMPLE: I don't think I can do this. (The apostrophe shows that the letter "o" has been left out.)

34. Use an apostrophe when you leave out the first two numbers of a year.

> EXAMPLE: She was in the class of '93.

35. For a singular noun that does not end in -*s*, add '*s*.

> EXAMPLE: The lady's hands were trembling.

36. For a one-syllable singular noun that ends in -*s*, add '*s*.

> EXAMPLE: It is my boss's birthday today.

37. If a singular noun has more than one syllable and ends in –s, it is acceptable to use only an apostrophe after the -s. (It is important to remain consistent.)

> EXAMPLE: The metropolis's citizens were very friendly during our visit.

> Acceptable: The metropolis' citizens were very friendly during our visit.

38. To form the possessive of a singular proper noun ending in -s, it is acceptable to add only an apostrophe. (It is important to remain consistent.)

> EXAMPLE: Mr. Ness's classroom is very inviting.

> Acceptable: Mr. Ness' classroom is very inviting.

39. If a plural noun ends in -s, add an apostrophe after the -s.

> EXAMPLE: The ladies' restroom was a mess.

40. If a plural noun does not end with an -s, form the possessive by using an apostrophe before an -s.

> EXAMPLE: The mice's tails were caught in a trap.

41. For a compound noun, place the possessive ending after the last word.

> EXAMPLE: My mother-in-law's car was in the garage during the hailstorm. (singular)

> EXAMPLE: My brothers-in-law's cars were damaged in the hailstorm. (plural)

42. To show possession of the same object by more than one noun, make only the last noun in the series possessive.

> EXAMPLE: I'm looking for Mrs. Garcia, Mrs. Lee, and Miss Carter's office. (They all share the same office.)

EXAMPLE: I'm looking for Mrs. Garcia's, Mrs. Lee's, and Miss Carter's offices. (Each person has her own office.)

43. Use an apostrophe to form the plural of a number, letter, sign, or word used as a word.

EXAMPLE: Check to see that you used the +'s and −'s correctly.

*QUOTATION MARKS

44. Use quotation marks before and after a direct quote. If the speaker tag interrupts the quoted material, then two sets of quotation marks are needed. However, do not put quotation marks around the speaker tag.

EXAMPLE: "I think my leg is broken," Jesse whimpered.

EXAMPLE: Did Mrs. Steele just say, "We are going to have a test today"?

EXAMPLE: "I can't move," Maria whispered. "I'm too scared."

45. Put quotation marks around the titles of short works, such as articles, songs, short stories, or poems.

EXAMPLE: Have you heard the song "Love Me Tender," by Elvis Presley?

46. Place quotation marks around words, letters, or symbols that are slang or being discussed or used in a special way.

EXAMPLE: I have a hard time spelling "miscellaneous."

47. Use single quotation marks for quotation marks within quotations.

> EXAMPLE: "Have you read the poem 'The Raven,' by Edgar Allan Poe?" I asked Chris.

48. Any punctuation used goes to the left of a quotation mark. However, if the punctuation is used to punctuate the whole sentence and not just what is inside the quotation marks, then it goes to the right.

> EXAMPLE: Have you read the poem "Annabel Lee"?

ELLIPSIS

49. Use an ellipsis to indicate a pause.

> EXAMPLE: You mean … I … uh … we have a test today?

50. Use an ellipsis to indicate omitted words in a quotation.

> EXAMPLE: "A great movie … full of … excitement."

51. If the ellipsis comes at the end of your sentence, you still need an end punctuation, even if it is a period.

> EXAMPLE: I started out my recitation of Lincoln's famous speech. "Four score and seven years ago…." After that, I forgot most of it.

HYPHEN

52. Use a hyphen in compound numbers from twenty-one to ninety-nine.

> EXAMPLE: The final score was seventy-eight to sixty-two.

53. Use a hyphen between the numbers in a fraction.

> EXAMPLE: I used only three-fourths of the flour you gave me.

54. Use a hyphen to form some compound words, especially compound adjectives that appear before the nouns they modify.

> EXAMPLE: The court took a ten-minute recess.

55. Use a hyphen to join a capital letter to a word.

> EXAMPLE: I had to have my arm X-rayed.

56. Use a hyphen to show a family relationship, except *grand*, *step*, and *half*.

> EXAMPLE: My sister-in-law helps take care of my great-aunt.

> EXAMPLE: We are going to go visit my grandparents while we are in town.

> EXAMPLE: Connie just found out that she has a half sister.

DASH

57. Use a pair of dashes to indicate a sudden interruption in a sentence. One handwritten dash is twice as long as a hyphen.

> EXAMPLE: There is one thing—actually there are several things—that I need to tell you.

58. Use a dash to attach an afterthought to an already complete sentence.

   EXAMPLE: Sarah bought a new pet yesterday—a boa constrictor.

59. Use a dash after a series of introductory elements.

   EXAMPLE: Murder, armed robbery, assault—he has a long list of felonies on his record.

PARENTHESES

60. Use a set of parentheses around a word or phrase in a sentence that adds information or makes an idea more clear.

   EXAMPLE: Your essay (all nine pages of it) is on my desk.

61. Do not use parentheses within parentheses. Use brackets in place of the inner parentheses.

   EXAMPLE: Please refer to *Julius Caesar* (Act IV, scene i [page 72]).

BRACKETS

62. Use brackets around words of your own that you add to the words of someone you are quoting.

   EXAMPLE: The news anchor announced, "It is my sad duty to inform our audience that we are now at war [with Iraq]."

*UNDERLINING (OR ITALICS) *It is better to use italics when available.*

63. Underline titles of long works such as books, magazines, albums, movies, etc. (Do not underline end punctuation.)

> EXAMPLE: We use <u>The Language Handbook</u> to study grammar.

> EXAMPLE: We use *The Language Handbook* to study grammar.

64. Underline foreign words that are not commonly used in everyday English.

> EXAMPLE: If you look closely, you'll see <u>e pluribus unum</u> on most U.S. currency.

> EXAMPLE: If you look closely, you'll see *e pluribus unum* on most U.S. currency.

65. Underline a word, number, or letter that is being discussed or used in a special way.

> EXAMPLE: Remember to dot every <u>i</u> and cross every <u>t</u>.

> EXAMPLE: Remember to dot every *i* and cross every *t*.

EXAMPLES OF PUNCTUATING TITLES CORRECTLY

UNDERLINE TITLES OF THE FOLLOWING:

- books   <u>Treasure Island</u>
- periodicals (magazines, newspapers)   <u>Time</u>, <u>The New York Times</u>
- long poems   <u>The Charge of the Light Brigade</u>
- plays   <u>The Phantom of the Opera</u>

■ movies/TV series   Spider-man, Monk
■ paintings/sculptures   The Birth of Venus, David
■ ships   Pequod

USE QUOTATION MARKS AROUND TITLES OF THE FOLLOWING:

■ short stories   "The Fun They Had"
■ chapter titles   "How to Choose a Topic"
■ essays   "Three Reasons to Love the Yankees"
■ articles in periodicals   "Storm of the Century"
■ short poems   "The Lanyard"
■ TV episodes   "Mr. Monk Goes to Vegas"
■ titles of web pages   "Academy of American Poets"
■ songs   "Positively Fourth Street"

REMEMBER: If a title is in *italics* (slanted type), it is already correct and does not need to be underlined or put inside quotation marks. Usually, titles that can be underlined can also be printed in *italics*.

EXAMPLES: *Treasure Island; Spider-man; The Phantom of the Opera*

CAPITALIZATION TIPS

Here are some general rules for using capital letters.

Use capital letters in the following ways:

1. The first words of a sentence

    EXAMPLE: The last train to Clarksville just left.

2. The pronoun *I*

    EXAMPLE: He thought that I was a good guitar player.

3. Proper nouns (the names of specific people, places, organizations, and sometimes things)

    EXAMPLES: Major League Baseball
    Empire State Building
    Syracuse, New York
    Lake Ontario
    Four H Club

4. Family titles (when used as proper names)

    EXAMPLE: I got Aunt Alice a book, and my other aunts got gift certificates.

    EXAMPLE: Where is Mother? Is she with your mother?

5. The names of religious figures and books.

    EXAMPLES: the Bible, God, Mohammed, Buddha, Moses

    Exception: Do not capitalize *god* if it's not specific. For example, "the Greek gods."

6. Titles preceding names

    EXAMPLE: Mayor LaGuardia was very popular.

7. Directions that are names (North, South, East, and West when used as sections of the country, but not as compass directions)

    EXAMPLE: We lived in the North all our lives.

    EXAMPLE: We hiked due south for three miles.

8. The days of the week, the months of the year, and holidays (but not the seasons used generally)

    EXAMPLES: Thanksgiving falls on the fourth Thursday in November.

    EXAMPLE: I love winter weather.

9. The names of countries, nationalities, and specific languages

    EXAMPLE: Great Britain, Australian, English

10. The first word in a sentence that is a direct quote

    EXAMPLE: Lincoln said, "Four score and seven years ago...."

11. The major words in the titles of books, articles, and songs (but not short prepositions or the articles *the*, *a*, or *an*, if they are not the first word of the title)

    EXAMPLE: I enjoyed reading *The Catcher Was a Spy.*

12. Members of national, political, racial, social, civic, and athletic groups

    EXAMPLES: New York Mets, African Americans, Republicans, Girl Scouts, Irish

13. Periods and events (but not century numbers)

    EXAMPLES: Ice Age, Great Depression, Presidential Election

    EXAMPLE: the twentieth century

14. Trademarks and company names

    EXAMPLE: Microsoft Word, General Electric

EDITING: PRACTICE EXERCISES

DIRECTIONS:

In each passage, there are some mistakes. You are to find the mistakes, cross them out and write in the correct answer. There are NO spelling errors.

1. *A Trip to the Toy Hall of Fame*

In june my class visited to the Toy Hall of Fame. We went to learn about the history of toys. We learned that toys help build physical and mental skills. We learned that they could educate while they entertain us. They saw an exhibit about what makes a toy good enough to be in the Toy Hall of Fame in Rochester NY. To be chosen a toy must be very popular. It must have been around for a long time. It should also be educational. Definitely needs to be safe, too.

2. *School Lunch*

Last week we had to make a graph for math class. So I take a survey of my class to see what their favoritest lunch is. The kids who brought their lunch to school thought peanut butter was the best to bring. Kids who bought there lunch in school liked peanut butter to, and brung peanut butter sandwiches two or three times a week.

I took the results from the survey and put them on the graph.

3. *The Wright Brothers*

Wilbur and Orville Wright they were the owners of a bicycle shop in Dayton ohio. They did not invent the airplane. Many people had try to fly, but they were the first to actually do it.

In December, 1903 at a place in North Carolina called Kitty Hawk, Wilbur flew there plane a total of 119 feet.

The flight last only 12 seconds, but because of the Wrights flight, they became famous as pioneers in aviation.

4. *Taking a Test*

Everybody in my class was nervous about taking our english test. Because our teacher wanted us to do well, they told us some things that would help us.

One thing was to be sure too read the questions carefully. That way we probably wouldnt make careless mistakes. An other thing we should do was pay attention to the directions and be sure to ask any questions we had before the test begun.

We learned that if we did these things, we would probably feel a lot more confident and would probably do better on the test.

5. *Playing Hockey*

Me and my friends like to play hockey. We live in a kinda cold part of the country, so there is plenty of ice to skate on in the Winter. We also have indoor ice rinks that are open all year, we have plenty of chances to practice.

Because we have so many chances to play and practice, our school has really good hockey.

6. *Leonardo da Vinci*

A lot of people have read a book called "The Da Vinci Code." It is a fiction book, but the man in the title Leonardo da Vinci, was a real person who lived in the 1500s.

He was born in the city of Vinci Italy, so his name really means "Leonardo of Vinci."

He was one of the smartest and most talented people which ever lived. He was an inventor, a painter, a sculptor, and a engineer. These were just a few of his talents.

His best-known painting were *The Last Supper*. He drew plans for such inventions as the helicopter, the parachute, the bicycle, and the printing press many years before they were actually built by other people.

SCORING THE EDITING PARAGRAPH

Courtesy of the New York State Department of Education.

SCORING RUBRIC: 3-POINT HOLISTIC EDITING TASK RUBRIC

3 points: No more than one error, either introduced or not corrected, remains after the student has corrected the passage.

2 points: Two to three errors, either introduced or not corrected, remain after the student has corrected the passage.

1 point: Four to five errors, either introduced or not corrected, remain after the student has corrected the passage.

0 points: Six or more errors, either introduced or not corrected, remain after the student has corrected the passage.

QUESTIONS AND ANSWERS ABOUT HOW THIS SECTION IS SCORED

Q: Will students be told how many errors are in the editing paragraph?

A: No, students should not be told how many errors to look for. Students might stop reviewing the rest of the paragraph because they believe they have found all the targeted errors when, in fact, they have misidentified one or more elements in the paragraph as being incorrect. It is best to encourage students always to review the entire paragraph.

Q: If a student changes a word in a paragraph, but the word is grammatically correct and fits the sentence, is that revision acceptable?

A: Such a revision is acceptable, provided that it does not alter the meaning of the sentence to such a degree that it no longer fits the context of the paragraph. This is an example of a neutral correction.

Q: What if a student has crossed out a serial comma before the word *and*?

A: Because the serial comma before *and* is considered optional, the change is treated as a neutral correction. The change does not make the sentence incorrect, and so it is permitted.

Q: Why have commas been included in the editing paragraphs?

A: Knowledge of commas is part of the New York State Learning Standards. Please refer to the English Language Arts Core Curriculum (Appendix 3) for grade-specific information.

Q: If a student creates a spelling error in the process of revising the paragraph, will the spelling error count against the student's score?

A: No. Because spelling is not assessed via the editing paragraph, spelling errors introduced by the student will not be counted either.

Q: Is the misuse of homophones (e.g., *to/too/two*) considered to be a spelling error or a usage error? Would a student be penalized for introducing a homophone error?

A: Homophones are considered usage errors. In grade 5, students will be held accountable for introducing such errors.

Q: If the error calls for a student to correct the tense of a verb, and the student misspells the new word, can that correction be given credit? (EXAMPLE: If *hear* should be corrected to *heard*, can *herd* be given credit?)

A: The correction should be given credit, provided that the word clearly and accurately represents the correction in tense despite the misspelling.

Q: Is a student permitted to cross out an entire sentence or part of a sentence rather than making the necessary correction? How much deleted text can be allowed?

A: A student is not permitted to cross out an entire sentence to avoid making a correction. If a student crosses out a small portion of a sentence, but the sentence is still grammatically intact and the meaning of the sentence remains unchanged, such a revision is acceptable.

Q: Will students be given credit for corrections made via the use of proofreading marks?

A: Proofreading marks will be allowed, provided that the errors are clearly indicated and corrected by the proofreading marks.

Q: If a student corrects an error by using means other than proofreading marks or the revision method described in the directions, will the response still receive credit?

A: If the correction is made clearly and accurately, full credit may be given. Some examples of acceptable corrections include the following:

- circling the error rather than crossing it out
- crossing out the part of the word that is incorrect rather than crossing out and rewriting the entire word
- crossing out an unnecessary punctuation mark rather than crossing out the preceding word and

punctuation mark and rewriting the word without the punctuation mark

■ directly inserting missing punctuation rather than crossing out the surrounding words and rewriting them above the crossed out section, with the correct punctuation inserted

In each of these cases, as long as the correction made is accurate and clear to the scorer, the correction is acceptable.

Q: Is a correction acceptable if a student makes the correction but does not cross out the original error?

A: Such a correction is acceptable, provided that the correction is completely clear, with no further interpretation necessary on the part of the scorer.

Q: If a student makes more than one error of a particular type (e.g., failing to capitalize a proper noun), is each instance considered an error, or are these errors grouped together and considered a single error?

A: In order to be considered a single error, the repeated error needs to be identical. For example, if a student repeatedly fails to capitalize a particular name, that is considered a single error, even though it occurs more than once. However, if the error occurs in two different names, then that is considered two separate errors.

Q: Is there a list of the types of errors that will be included in the editing paragraphs?

A: Although there is no comprehensive list of assessable errors, the English Language Arts Learning Standards and the Core Curriculum (Appendix 3) provide guidelines regarding grade-specific content coverage, and the Sample Test provides examples of grade-level-appropriate concepts.

Chapter 5

GLOSSARY

IMPORTANT TERMS FOR RESPONDING TO TEST QUESTIONS

Antonym
A word with an opposite, or almost opposite meaning as another.

> EXAMPLE: *Down* is an antonym of *up*. *Loud* is an antonym of *quiet*.

Autobiography
The story of a person's life written by himself or herself

Biography
The story of a person's life written by someone other than the person written about

Blank Verse
A poem that does not rhyme

Cause and Effect
The *cause* of something is what makes it happen. The *effect* is what happens.

> EXAMPLE: I stepped on the brake and my car stopped. Stepping on the brake was the *cause*, and my car stopping was the *effect*.

Character

A person, spirit, object, animal, or natural force in a story. Anything that can provide action in the story can be a character.

Characterization

The method a writer uses to tell the reader about a character in a story. This may be done (1) by what the character says about himself or herself; (2) by what others say or show about the character; and (3) by the character's own actions.

Climax

The "high point" in a story. It is the peak of the action. It is when we learn whether the main character will succeed or fail at what he/she is trying to do.

Comparison

This is a technique where authors *compare* two things. That is, they show how things are *similar* (alike) or *different*. Sometimes the term *contrast* is used to talk about differences.

> EXAMPLE: Frodo and Gollum are similar because they both want the ring. They are different because Frodo is good and Gollum is evil.

Conclusion (or **Resolution**)

The conclusion is the logical outcome of the story. It is how the story "turns out."

Conflict

Conflict occurs when the protagonist (main character) is opposed by some person or force in the story. The most usual conflicts are

- person vs. person
- person vs. self

- person vs. nature
- person vs. society
- person vs. the supernatural/unknown

Context
This is the background or situation of the passage. Think of it as a combination of the *setting* and the *plot.*

Context Clues
Information and details from the context that can be used to figure out word meanings or to make inferences about parts of the story

Dialogue
In drama, a conversation between characters

Fable
A brief tale designed to illustrate a moral lesson. Often the characters are animals, as in the fables of Aesop.

Fact
Something that can be proven to be true

> EXAMPLES: 2 + 2 = 4; George Washington was our first president.

Figurative Language
In literature, this is a way of saying one thing and meaning something else. Similes, metaphors, personification, and hyperbole (high *per* bo lee) are *figures of speech* that are based on comparisons.

Figure of Speech
An example of figurative language that says something that is not literally (exactly) true in order to create an effect in the story

Flashback
A reference to an event that took place before the beginning of a story or play.

Many stories start in the present but most of the action is seen as a flashback.

Foreshadowing
Hints or clues about what is going to happen later in a story

Free Verse
Unrhymed poetry with lines of varying lengths. It might sound like prose.

Genre
The type of story. Some genres you have read are fiction, nonfiction, poetry, and plays.

Haiku
A form of Japanese poetry that usually has three lines and a maximum of 17 syllables. The poems do not rhyme, and are often about nature.

Hyperbole
A figure of speech where there is *exaggeration* (making something sound bigger, more important, older, etc., than it really is)

> EXAMPLE: "I've told you a million times to take out the trash."

Imagery
A word or group of words in a story that connect to one or more of the senses: sight, taste, touch, hearing, and smell. The use of imagery helps the author to SHOW rather than TELL.

Implication (imply)
A hint or suggestion. It is information that is not directly stated, and can be figured out by making an Inference. (See next term.)

EXAMPLE: When your teacher says, "Study your notes very well tonight," he or she is probably *implying* that there will be a quiz tomorrow.

Inference (infer)
A conclusion based on your knowledge or experience

EXAMPLE: When your teacher says, "Study your notes very well tonight," you will probably *infer* (based on your experience) that there will be a quiz tomorrow.

Irony
The opposite of what is expected or appropriate (what "should" happen)

Snow in July would be unexpected but **not** ironic. Snowing so much in winter that the ski club has to cancel a ski trip **would** be ironic.

Literal (literally)
Exact; specific (exactly; specifically)

EXAMPLE: When someone says, "Get lost," they do not want you to literally lose yourself. They want you to go away.

Metaphor
A figure of speech that makes a comparison between two unlike things *without* using the words *like* or *as*

EXAMPLE: "The linebacker is a real moose."

Mood
The feeling created in a story. Moods such as horror, suspense, sadness, anger, humor, inspiration, etc., may be a result of the characters' words and actions, the setting, or description by the narrator.

Narrative Poem
A poem that tells a story. Narrative poems are usually long, sometimes even book length.

Narrator
The one who tells the story. The narrator can be in the story or outside it. (See Point of View.)

Novel
A long fictional prose work

Opinion
An opinion is someone's point of view or way of looking at something. An opinion cannot be considered a fact, even though it *may* be true.

> EXAMPLE: "Chocolate ice cream is the best" is an opinion, but there is no way to prove that it is true. "The Yankees are the best team in baseball" is an opinion. Even though it might be true, there is no way to prove it is a fact.

Personification
A figure of speech in which something that is not human is given human characteristics

> EXAMPLE: The wind whistled. The birds chattered.

Plot
The action of a story. The plot is what happens in a story. It usually involves some kind of conflict. Plot usually refers to what the story is *about*.

Poetry
Poetry is a type of writing that usually uses language in a much richer way than prose, often with rhythm, rhyme, imagery, and figures of speech. Poems are usually laid out in separate lines, so that the breaks come where the poet chooses rather than where typical sentence structure might put them.

Point of View
This is "where" the narrator is telling the story. The narrator is either in the story (FIRST PERSON) or outside the story (THIRD PERSON).

Purpose
The author's reason for writing the piece. This might be to persuade, inform, entertain, amuse, etc.

Prose
This is "regular" writing, the writing we do most of the time. It is composed of sentences and paragraphs. Most of the reading we do is prose.

Protagonist
The main character of a story. The opposite character is the antagonist, who creates conflict for the main character.

Rhyme
In poetry, it is the pattern of repeated sounds.

In end rhyme, the rhyme is at the end of the line.

In internal rhyme, the rhyme words are in a place in the line instead of at the end.

Rhythm
Some poems (like songs) often have a beat or sound pattern called *rhythm*.

Sequence
The order in which events take place. Most things that are done in steps are said to be in a sequence.

> EXAMPLE: I ate my salad, and then I ate my burger. Finally I had dessert.

Setting
The time and place of a story. It is when and where the story happens. It may be told to the reader or he/she might have to make an *inference* about it.

Short Story
A short fictional narrative. Novels are long, whereas short stories are exactly what the name says: **short** stories.

Simile
A figure of speech that compares two things that are not alike, but have some features that are alike *(similarities)*. Similes use the words *like* or *as*.

> EXAMPLE: The student jumped up and down like a rubber ball.

Stanza
A division (or section) of a poem. It is similar to a paragraph in prose writing.

Structure
The way a story is "put together" or organized

Symbolism
This is the use of an object to represent an idea.

EXAMPLE: A picture of a heart is often used to represent emotions such as love or sadness.

Synonym
A word with the same or nearly the same meaning as another.

EXAMPLE: *Correct* is a synonym for *right*. *Over* is a synonym for *above*.

Theme
The theme is the message, moral, main idea, or lesson that the author wants to get across. Don't confuse it with the *plot*.

Tone
Tone expresses the author's attitude (feelings) about his or her subject. For example, a story can have a humorous tone, a mysterious tone, a serious tone, etc.

ANSWERS AND EXPLANATION FOR PRACTICE EXERCISES IN CHAPTERS 1, 2, 3, 4

READING COMPREHENSION

ANSWERS AND EXPLANATIONS

Following are the answers to the practice questions and explanations about how the answers might be found. Explanations for terms in **bold** print may be found on the list of terms in Chapter 2.

Practice Exercise 1

Larry Doby: There's Nothing Wrong with Being Second

1. Which of the following is most likely the author's purpose for writing this piece?

   A. to show which of the two players was better

   B. to pay tribute to Larry Doby

   C. to tell what a good player Larry Doby was

   D. to tell what a good player Jackie Robinson was

This is a **MAIN IDEA** question. Answers A, C and D can be eliminated because the passage does not mention the specific playing skills of either player. To "pay tribute" means to praise or say good things about someone, and that is what the passage does.

2. In the first sentence, the word *pioneer* most likely means

   A. an early settler of the Old West

   B. the first person to perform a historic task

   C. a person known for his athletic skill

   D. a person who became famous

You probably know that *pioneers* settled the Old West, but they did that because they were the first to perform that historic task. Because this passage is NOT about settling the Old West, and says that Jackie Robinson was the FIRST African American major leaguer (certainly a historic task), you can *INFER* that **(B.) the first person to perform a historic task** is correct.

3. Besides being the second African American player, he was also the second African American

   A. pitcher

   B. owner

   C. broadcaster

   D. manager

This is a **FACT-BASED** question, and the answer **(D.) manager** is given to you in the last paragraph.

4. As used in the second paragraph, the word *debut* refers to Jackie Robinson's

   A. first game

   B. last game

   C. best game

   D. worst game

You can figure this out using **CONTEXT CLUES.** Since it is said that Robinson was the first African American to play major-league baseball, and he *started* in 1947, 11 weeks before Larry Doby, you can **INFER** that Doby started playing eleven weeks after Robinson's (A.) first game—his *debut*.

Practice Exercise 2

Not as Smart as We Thought

5. In the last paragraph it says, "The three guilty rocketeers realized just what had happened." What had happened?

    A. They had managed to fool the science teacher.

    B. They had managed to fool the English teacher.

    C. They had been outsmarted by their teacher.

    D. They received a good grade on the project.

This is a **FACT-BASED** question. It is obvious that the author thought they had fooled the teacher, but it turned out that she knew who had done the "rocket launching" because she called only in the three "guilty rocketeers." Therefore, (C.) they had been outsmarted by their teacher.

6. The author's purpose in writing this story was most likely to

    A. show how smart the boys were in English and science

    B. show how sneaky the boys were in class

    C. show how a good teacher handles a problem

    D. show how to get away with mischief in school

This is a **MAIN IDEA** and **INFERENCE** question, which really asks what the author wanted to tell us. Because it is about how the boys learned a lesson about teachers, the author's purpose would be to show us how the teacher let the "guilty rocketeers" resolve the problem themselves. So, (C.) **show how a good teacher handles a problem** is the correct answer.

7.   According to the story, another good title for it might be

   A. "Teachers Are Always Right"

   B. "An Interesting Punishment"

   C. "Good Boys Gone Bad"

   D. "A Clever Solution"

This is a **BEST TITLE** kind of question. The story shows just how clever (smart) the teacher is by the way she handles the problem (the solution). It was (D.) "A Clever Solution."

8.   What might be a reason that Mrs. C didn't punish the boys?

   A. she hadn't caught them doing it

   B. she wasn't sure they were guilty

   C. she liked their clever invention

   D. she knew her way would work better

You may get this answer by making **INFERENCES.** In the last paragraph it is clear that she knew who had been shooting the paper rockets and allowed the boys to figure out that she knew. She knew they would not repeat the bad behavior, so there was no reason to punish them for a first offense.

Practice Exercise 3

Getting There Was Not Easy

9. According to the story, "to look up to someone" **most likely** means

    A. to understand him

    B. to know him

    C. to like him

    D. to dislike him

The author implied that they would already have to look up to Shaq because he was tall. You would **INFER** the meaning **(C.) to like him** because Shaq thought his behavior might help him make friends.

10. According to the story, Shaquille O'Neal's parents **most likely** wanted Shaq to become

    A. a good basketball player

    B. a good student

    C. a good person

    D. a good joker

This is an **INFERENCE** question. In paragraph 4, the author writes, "It was definitely not the kind of behavior that his parents wanted for him. They wanted him to follow The Golden Rule: to treat others as he would like to be treated." Someone who did that would most likely turn out to be **(C.) a good person**.

11. In the second paragraph the word *peers* refers to

   A. his fellow students

   B. his teachers and administrators

   C. his coaches and teachers

   D. his parents and teachers

   You can get this answer using CONTEXT CLUES and INFERENCE. The author is talking about Shaq being ignored by people he seemed to want to make friends with. Because he was thirteen, it would make sense that (A.) his fellow students would be those people he called his peers.

12. The author probably wrote this story to give advice to

   A. basketball fans

   B. basketball players

   C. practical jokers

   D. young people

   This is a MAIN IDEA and AUTHOR'S PURPOSE question. He is definitely giving good advice and since he is talking about a time when Shaquille was a young person ("When he was 13...") and about how he behaved then, the INFERENCE is that the audience for the piece is (D.) young people.

Practice Exercise 4

From Country Veterinarian to Famous Author

13. A "pen name" is a name chosen to be used by

   A. a veterinarian

   B. a farmer

   C. an author

   D. an animal

   This question requires you to use CONTEXT CLUES to figure it out. "James Herriot" was the name James Alfred Wight chose to use when he wrote his books. Another great clue would be that author would probably use a pen to write. So, (C.) **an author** would be the best answer.

14. What did James Herriot NOT do?

   A. grow up in Scotland

   B. become an author

   C. work in a large city

   D. work with horses

   This is a FACT-BASED question. You need to find the three things he DID do in order to discover the one he DID NOT do. The story says that he grew up in Scotland (A), became an author (B), and worked with horses (D). It does not say that he (C.) **worked in a large city**.

15. As used in this story, the term *delivering* refers to

   A. bringing mail to people on farms

   B. helping with the birth of animals

   C. doing good deeds in school

   D. working for a veterinarian

This is a **VOCABULARY** question. You can use **CONTEXT CLUES** to get the answer. "He worked mostly with large animals," so "delivering" or (B.) helping with the birth of animals would be a big part of his job.

16. Which did Mr. Herriot do last?

    A. worked as a veterinarian for dogs

    B. wrote about his work with animals

    C. attended college in Glasgow

    D. dreamed about being a veterinarian

This is a simple **SEQUENCE** question. The story includes each of the answers and shows the order in which they happened. The last of the events was that he (B.) wrote about his work with animals.

Practice Exercise 5

The Main Street Elementary School Fourth-Grade Girls Free-Throw Shooting Contest Overtime Sudden Victory Shootout

17. This is a narrative poem because it

    A. uses poetic devices

    B. tells a story

    C. creates a mood

    D. turns out happy

This is partly a **VOCABULARY** question, because the definition of a narrative poem is that it (B.) tells a story. By reading the poem it is clear that it does tell a story.

18. The words "CLANG" and "SWISH" describe

   A. calls made by the referee

   B. noises made by the crowd

   C. sounds made by the scoreboard

   D. sounds made by the basketball

The **INFERENCE** you would make is that because these noises are made when the basketball hits something (D.) sounds made by the basketball would be correct.

19. The phrase *gymnasium's silent air* is an example of which poetic device?

   A. simile

   B. hyperbole

   C. metaphor

   D. foreshadowing

By knowing the **MEANING** of (C.) metaphor, you would know that *gymnasium's silent air* is a direct comparison. It is used to show that the crowd was quiet, maybe holding their breath. Also, sometimes you can **ELIMINATE** obviously incorrect answers to get the correct one, so if you know that none of the others are correct, you could arrive at the correct answer.

20. The poet creates a mood in the poem that is best described as

   A. happy

   B. sad

   C. relaxed

   D. tense

An **INFERENCE** from the FACTS that Rebecca said she had fun, that her grandfather saw her shot in a good way even though she missed, and that he said they had both won, makes (A.) **happy** the best answer.

21. The poet **most likely** capitalized some of the words

    A. because they are supposed to be

    B. because he was careless

    C. to make them seem important

    D. to make them interesting

Your **INFERENCE** that **(C.) to make them seem important** would be correct. They are all sounds and actions that were an important part of the two basketball shots.

LISTENING SECTION

ANSWERS AND EXPLANATIONS

Practice Exercise—Passage 1

1. One-room schoolhouses were the backbone of education in Bland County. As it is used in this passage, the word *backbone* most nearly means

    A. the main part

    B. one of several kinds

    C. a new type of building

    D. a problem

This is a **VOCABULARY/INFERENCE** question. Since the passage is all about the one-room school, it is obviously very important. We don't know that there are several kinds of education, it is not in a new type of building, and there is nothing about it being a problem. Therefore, **(A.) the main part** is the best choice.

2. According to the passage, the word *ruckus* most nearly means

 A. snowstorm

 B. illness

 C. disturbance

 D. test

This is a **VOCABULARY/INFERENCE** question. The teacher is talking about punishment, so the only one of the choices that would lead to someone being punished would be (**C.**) **disturbance** in the classroom.

3. Based on the information in the passage, Liberty School was most likely located

 A. in a city

 B. in the country

 C. in the desert

 D. in a resort

This is an **INFERENCE** question. Because it is not directly told to us in the story, we need to use clues and our own knowledge. Students walked or rode horses, chopped wood to heat the school, and drank water from a bucket. These are all things most closely associated with country life (**B.**).

4. According to the passage, which subject was not taught until the upper grades?

 A. reading

 B. writing

 C. arithmetic

 D. science

This is a FACT-BASED question. In the first paragraph it tells us that (D.) science was not taught until the upper grades.

5. A teacher in a one-room school would have to know how to

    A. teach many subjects

    B. chop firewood

    C. drive a school bus

    D. coach baseball

This is an INFERENCE question. There were no school buses and baseball is not mentioned. A teacher *might* need to be able to chop wood, but since there was only one teacher and many subjects, (A.) teach many subjects is the best answer.

Practice Exercise—Passage 2

6. The Oz Fest is most likely in Chittenango because

    A. it is Dorothy's hometown

    B. it is L. Frank Baum's hometown

    C. *The Wizard of Oz* was filmed there

    D. it used to be called "Oz."

This is an INFERENCE/FACT-BASED question. It would be logical to infer that (B.) it is L. Frank Baum's hometown is correct. Also, none of the other answers appear in the passage.

7. L. Frank Baum's books started out as

   A. stories he told his friends

   B. the diary he wrote in the army

   C. stories to entertain his children

   D. a movie he saw in Hollywood

This is a FACT-BASED question. We are told that he made up the (C.) stories to entertain his children.

8. How many *Oz* books were published AFTER *The Wonderful Wizard of Oz?*

   A. 10

   B. 11

   C. 12

   D. 13

This is a FACT-BASED question. We are told that he "wrote (D.) thirteen more books about the people of the Land of Oz."

9. L. Frank Baum was probably able to write so many children's book because he

   A. had a good typewriter

   B. believed in witches

   C. had a good imagination

   D. had plenty of spare time

This is an INFERENCE question. We know from our own experience that it takes great imagination to write fantasy stories about magical imaginary characters. Even if he had a good typewriter and spare time, his (C.) imagination would be the most important thing for creating the stories themselves.

10. According to the passage, the 1939 movie *The Wizard of Oz* was most likely popular because

A. it was in color

B. it had good actors

C. children loved it

D. the effects were realistic

This is an **INFERENCE** question. We are told that the movie Baum made in 1914 was not successful because children didn't get to see it. We know that children still love the 1939 version almost 70 years later. So, the fact that (C.) **children loved it** would most likely be the reason it was so popular.

Practice Exercise—Passage 3

11. As used in the passage, the word *glaze* most nearly means a

A. coating for the outside

B. flavoring for the center

C. hardener for the shell

D. softener for the jelly

This is an **INFERENCE** question. Because the glaze is added to give the beans a shiny look, it would have to be a (A.) **coating for the outside**, where it could be seen.

12. Since 1976, there have been

A. two types of jelly beans

B. two different flavors

C. two new ingredients

D. two different prices

This is a FACT-BASED question. The answer is in the first sentence of paragraph 8. In taking notes, the year 1976 should stand out as a KEY WORD, and signal a good place to look for the answer, (A.) two types of jelly beans.

13. Jelly beans became associated with Easter mostly because of their

   A. size

   B. cost

   C. taste

   D. shape

This is a FACT-BASED question. "Easter" would be a key word in notetaking, because it is a holiday. That would make you focus on the connection between Easter and jelly beans, and the answer (D) shape is found there.

14. According to the passage, one way that gourmet jelly beans are different from traditional jelly beans is that they are

   A. cheaper

   B. smaller

   C. better

   D. cleaner

This is a FACT-BASED question that COMPARES the two kinds of jelly beans. In lines 3 and 4 of paragraph 8, it gives two ways they are different. Only one, (B.) smaller is a possible choice.

15. According to the passage, the most likely reason that jelly beans are still popular today is that they are

   A. long lasting

   B. easy to carry

   C. part of Easter

   D. good tasting

   This is an **INFERENCE/CONCLUSION** question. You know that jelly beans are candy and that they have been around for a very long time. Since you also know that the best reason that candy is popular is its good taste, so (**D.**) good tasting is the best.

16. Another good title for this passage would be

   A. "An Easter Tradition"

   B. "My Favorite Candy"

   C. "The History of Jelly Beans"

   D. "Candy Making in France"

   Because the title of a piece usually refers to its main idea or purpose, you need to ask yourself what the writing is **MOSTLY ABOUT.** This piece is mostly about (**C.**) "The History of Jelly Beans" since it tells about them from their beginnings a very long time ago.

Practice Exercise—Passage 4

17. According to the story, we know that Moe Berg spoke

   A. Dutch

   B. Japanese

   C. Russian

   D. Swedish

This is a FACT-BASED/INFERENCE question. We are told that he delivered a speech in Japan in (B.) **Japanese.** None of the other languages are mentioned in the story.

18. According to the story, we know that Moe traveled to each country EXCEPT

    A. Yugoslavia

    B. Germany

    C. Brazil

    D. Japan

This is also a FACT-BASED question, where we must find the three countries we know he did visit in order to know the one he didn't. We are told that he traveled to Yugoslavia (as a spy, by parachute), to Germany (also as a spy) and to Japan (as a ballplayer and spy). (C.) **Brazil** is not mentioned in the passage.

19. As it is used in the story, the word *brilliant* most closely means

    A. athletic

    B. intelligent

    C. modest

    D. generous

This is a VOCABULARY/INFERENCE question, where we use the CONTEXT to find the correct answer. Since the sentence is about his accomplishment as a student (finishing second in his class even though he had a very busy schedule) and we know that he had already shown how intelligent he was in other schools, it is the correct choice. Even though he had also shown that he was athletic, (B.) **intelligent** is the better of the two.

20. According to the story, Moe Berg definitely played for what major-league teams?

A. Giants and Yankees

B. Dodgers and Yankees

C. Yankees and White Sox

D. Dodgers and White Sox

This is a FACT-BASED/INFERENCE question. We know he played for the Brooklyn Dodgers, the Chicago White Sox, and as a reserve for *three more* teams, but they aren't named. Therefore, the answer is (D.) Dodgers and White Sox.

21. Another good title for this story would be

A. "A Brave and Talented Man"

B. "How to Learn a Foreign Language"

C. "Babe Ruth's Friend"

D. "A Dangerous Job"

This is a BEST TITLE kind of question, where we must decide what the passage is MOSTLY ABOUT. The passage does not tell how to learn a foreign language. He probably was Babe Ruth's friend, and spying is definitely a dangerous job, but the passage is MOSTLY about how talented and brave he was, so that (A.) "A Brave and Talented Man" would make the best title.

SHORT RESPONSE

ANSWERS AND EXPLANATIONS

As you go over the answers, it may be helpful to look back at the WWWWWH chart to see how the information applies to each passage.

Practice Exercise—Passage 1

There's Nothing Wrong with Being Second

QUESTION: *Use details from the passage to show why the title is a good one.*

Possible correct responses:

- Even though Larry Doby was second, he still played in the major leagues.
- He was actually the first African American in the American League.
- He had a successful career.
- He became a major-league manager.
- He was elected to the Baseball Hall of Fame.

Any other correct responses are also acceptable.

Practice Exercise—Passage 2

The Main Street Elementary School Fourth-Grade Girls Free-Throw Shooting Contest Overtime Sudden Victory Shootout

QUESTION: *Use details from the poem to show why the poet says they "both had won."*

Possible correct responses:

- He "saw" his granddaughter doing everything right when she made the shot.
- He "saw" and "heard" the ball going through the net.
- She told him that she had had fun.
- He was glad that she thought having fun was more important than winning.
- He didn't care that she had not won the shootout.

Any other correct responses are also acceptable.

Practice Exercise—Passage 3

From Country Veterinarian to Famous Author

QUESTION: *Using information from the passage, explain three things that Alf Wight did that helped him become the famous writer, James Herriot.*

Possible correct responses:

- He went to high school.
- He went to college.
- He decided to become a veterinarian.
- He worked as a veterinarian in Yorkshire.
- He worked with large farm animals.
- He worked with small animals too.
- He wrote down his adventures with animals.
- He chose the pen name James Herriot.

Any other correct responses are also acceptable.

Practice Exercise—Passage 4

A Very Old Candy

QUESTION: *Using details from the passage, compare the old and new ways of making jelly beans.*

Possible correct responses:

- There was a Mid-Eastern candy called Turkish Delight.
- The French made a candy called Jordan Almonds.
- They coated almonds with sugar and syrup in bowls.
- Eventually the two candies were combined.
- These early jelly beans were made by hand.
- The process is done by machines today.
- Jelly bean makers start with the center of the jelly bean.
- Sugar, corn syrup, and other ingredients are cooked in large vats.
- The mixture is put into molds to harden.
- A shiny glaze is added.
- In America, jelly beans became a very popular "penny candy."

Any other correct responses are also acceptable.

Practice Exercise—Passage 5

Down the Real Yellow Brick Road

QUESTION: *Using details from the passage, tell how L. Frank Baum's real life made the Oz Fest possible.*

Possible correct responses:

- Lyman Frank Baum was born in Chittenango in 1857.

- He started writing when he was young.
- His father gave him a printing press and he and his brother Henry started a newspaper.
- While he traveled, he made up stories to entertain his children.
- He published several books. That allowed him to stop traveling and spend his time writing more books.
- In 1900, he published *The Wonderful Wizard of Oz*.
- This is the book that made him famous.
- He continued to write children's books.
- He became a very successful writer and publisher.
- In 1939, the movie we know as simply *The Wizard of Oz* was released.
- It has become one of the most popular movies of all time.
- Children *and* adults love it even today, nearly seventy years later.

Any other correct responses are also acceptable.

EDITING SECTION

ANSWERS AND EXPLANATIONS

Practice Exercise—Passage 1

1. *A Trip to the Toy Hall of Fame*

In june my class visited to the Toy Hall of Fame. We went to learn about the history of toys. We learned that toys help build physical and mental skills. We learned that they could educate while they entertain us. They saw an exhibit about what makes a toy good enough to be in the Toy Hall of Fame in Rochester NY. To be chosen a toy must be very popular. It must have been around for a long time.

It should also be educational. Definitely needs to be safe, too.

Answers

Line 1: "June" should be capitalized because it is the name of a month.

Line 1: The expression "visited to" is incorrect usage. It should be corrected to:

- ■ my class visited the Toy Hall of Fame

OR

- ■ my class went to the Toy Hall of Fame

OR

- ■ my class made a visit to the Toy Hall of Fame

OR

- ■ Any other correct revision would be acceptable.

Line 4: "They saw an exhibit…" should be "We saw an exhibit…" because the person writing the piece was part of the group.

Line 6: There should be a comma separating the name of the city and state:

- ■ Rochester, NY

Lines 8 and 9: "Definitely needs to be safe, too." is a sentence fragment. There needs to be a subject in the sentence. It may be corrected more than one way:

- ■ It definitely…

OR

- A toy definitely…

OR

- Any other correct revision would be acceptable.

2. *School Lunch*

Last week we had to make a graph for math class. So I take a survey of my class to see what their favoritest lunch is. The kids who brought their lunch to school thought peanut butter was the best to bring. Kids who bought there lunch in school liked peanut butter to, and brung peanut butter sandwiches two or three times a week.

I took the results from the survey and put them on the graph.

Answers

Lines 1, 2, and 3: The second sentence, "So I take a survey of my class to see what their favoritest lunch is," has three errors.

First, it is a fragment that may be corrected by making the following changes:

- Putting a comma after "So." So, I take a survey of my class to see what their favoritest lunch is."

OR

- Eliminating the word "So." I take a survey of my class to see what their favoritest lunch is."

OR

- Combining it with the first sentence: Last week we had to make a graph for math class, so I take a survey of my class to see what their favoritest lunch is.

Second, the word "take" is present tense and the action is past tense, so the word "took" should be used instead.

Third, there is no correct word "favoritest." "Favorite" or even "most favorite" would be correct.

Line 5: The usage "there lunch" is possessive, so it should be "their lunch."

Line 5: The word "to" should be "too," meaning "also."

Line 5: The word "brung" is never correct. "Brought" would be the best choice. "Took," is a weak choice, but could be considered correct.

3. *The Wright Brothers*

Wilbur and Orville Wright they were the owners of a bicycle shop in Dayton ohio. They did not invent the airplane. Many people had try to fly, but they were the first to actually do it.

In December, 1903 at a place in North Carolina called Kitty Hawk, Wilbur flew there plane a total of 119 feet.

The flight last only 12 seconds, but because of the Wrights flight, they became famous as pioneers in aviation.

Answers

Line 1: Cross out the word "they." It is incorrect usage.

Line 2: There should be a comma between the city and state: Dayton, Ohio.

Line 2: Capitalize the names of states: Ohio

Line 3: The expression "had try" is incorrect tense agreement. "had tried" would be the best choice, "tried" would be correct, but not as good.

Line 5: Cross out the comma in "December, 1903." No comma is used if there is only the month and year given.

Line 6: To say "there plane" is incorrect. It is a possessive, so the word "their" should be used.

Line 7: Change the word "last." It needs to be the past tense, "lasted."

Line 7: The word "Wrights" is possessive, so it should have an apostrophe: Either "Wrights'" (preferred choice) or "Wrights's" would be correct.

4. *Taking a Test*

Everybody in my class was nervous about taking our english test. Because our teacher wanted us to do well, they told us some things that would help us.

One thing was to be sure to read the questions carefully. That way we probably wouldnt make careless mistakes. An other thing we should do was pay attention to the directions and be sure to ask any questions we had before the test begun.

We learned that if we did these things, we would probably feel a lot more confident and would probably do better on the test.

Answers

Line 2: The word "english" is incorrect. "English" should always be capitalized because it in the name of a language.

Lines 2 and 3: "Teacher" is singular and "they" is plural. They must both be the same number, so you could fix the sentence in different ways:

- Because our teachers wanted us to do well, they told us some things that would help us.

OR

- Because our teacher wanted us to do well, she told us some things that would help us.

OR

- Because our teacher wanted us to do well, he told us some things that would help us.

OR

- Any other correct revision would be acceptable.

Line 5: The contraction wouldnt is incorrect. It needs an apostrophe to replace the missing "o" in "not." It should be written "wouldn't."

Line 6: "An" and "other" should be one word – "Another."

Line 8: The word "begun" is incorrect. The word "began" should be used because it is the past tense of "begin."

5. *Playing Hockey*

Me and my friends like to play hockey. We live in a kinda cold part of the country, so there is plenty of ice to skate on in the Winter. We also have indoor ice rinks that are open all year, we have plenty of chances to practice.

Because we have so many chances to play and practice, our school has really good hockey.

Answers

Line 1, sentence 1: "My friends and I like to play hockey." "Me and my friends" is incorrect usage. Always put yourself last when there is more than one person in a list.

Line 1, sentence 2: The word "kinda" is not correct. The sentence could be changed to:

- We live in a cold part of the country

OR

- We live in kind of a cold part of the country

OR

- anything that corrects the expression "kinda."

Line 3: "Winter" is incorrect. The names of seasons are not capitalized unless they begin a sentence or are part of a title. The correct word here is "winter."

Lines 3 and 4: The sentence "We also have indoor ice rinks that are open all year, we have plenty of chances to practice," is incorrect. It is a run on sentence that could be fixed in more than one way:

- Because we also have indoor ice rinks that are open all year, we have plenty of chances to practice.

OR

- We also have indoor ice rinks that are open all year, so we have plenty of chances to practice.

OR

- We also have indoor ice rinks that are open all year. We have plenty of chances to practice.

OR

- Any other correct revision would be acceptable.

NOTE: Lines 5 and 6: This is a rather awkward statement. It implies that:

- Because we have so many chances to play and practice, our school has really good hockey teams.

OR

- Because we have so many chances to play and practice, our school has a really good hockey team.

IMPORTANT POINT: This is the type of change a student might make that actually goes from one correct form to another correct form. The directions say that responses are incorrect if they fail to correct a mistake or if they introduce a new mistake. Therefore, neither of these changes would be incorrect, since they are only "correcting" something that is already correct and have not introduced a new error.

6. *Leonardo da Vinci*

A lot of people have read a book called "The Da Vinci Code." It is a fiction book, but the man in the title Leonardo da Vinci, was a real person who lived in the 1500s.

He was born in the city of Vinci Italy, so his name really means "Leonardo of Vinci."

He was one of the smartest and most talented people which ever lived. He was an inventor, a painter, a sculptor, and a engineer. These were just a few of his talents.

His best-known painting were *The Last Supper*. He drew plans for such inventions as the helicopter, the parachute, the bicycle, and the printing press many years before they were actually built by other people.

Answers

Lines 1 and 2: <u>The Da Vinci Code</u> should be underlined, not in quotation marks, because it is a book. If it had been printed in italics, *The Da Vinci Code,* it would have been correct and you would not change it.

Line 2: There should be a comma between the words "title" and "Leonardo."

Line 5: There should be a comma between the words "Vinci" and "Italy" because there must be a comma between the name of a city and its country.

Line 8: The word "which" should be changed to "who" because the sentence is about a person.

Line 9: The term "a engineer" should be changed to "an engineer." The word "an" must be used before a vowel sound.

Line 10: The sentence should be: "His best known painting was the *The Last Supper.*" Since "painting" is singular, the word "was" must be used.

PRACTICE TEST 1—ANSWER SHEET

1. Ⓐ Ⓑ Ⓒ Ⓓ   8. Ⓐ Ⓑ Ⓒ Ⓓ   15. Ⓐ Ⓑ Ⓒ Ⓓ

2. Ⓐ Ⓑ Ⓒ Ⓓ   9. Ⓐ Ⓑ Ⓒ Ⓓ   16. Ⓐ Ⓑ Ⓒ Ⓓ

3. Ⓐ Ⓑ Ⓒ Ⓓ   10. Ⓐ Ⓑ Ⓒ Ⓓ   17. Ⓐ Ⓑ Ⓒ Ⓓ

4. Ⓐ Ⓑ Ⓒ Ⓓ   11. Ⓐ Ⓑ Ⓒ Ⓓ   18. Ⓐ Ⓑ Ⓒ Ⓓ

5. Ⓐ Ⓑ Ⓒ Ⓓ   12. Ⓐ Ⓑ Ⓒ Ⓓ   19. Ⓐ Ⓑ Ⓒ Ⓓ

6. Ⓐ Ⓑ Ⓒ Ⓓ   13. Ⓐ Ⓑ Ⓒ Ⓓ   20. Ⓐ Ⓑ Ⓒ Ⓓ

7. Ⓐ Ⓑ Ⓒ Ⓓ   14. Ⓐ Ⓑ Ⓒ Ⓓ

21. _____

_____

_____

_____

22. Ⓐ Ⓑ Ⓒ Ⓓ

23. Ⓐ Ⓑ Ⓒ Ⓓ

24. Ⓐ Ⓑ Ⓒ Ⓓ

25. Ⓐ Ⓑ Ⓒ Ⓓ

26. _____

_____

_____

_____

PRACTICE TEST ONE

PART 1—READING COMPREHENSION

Read the following passages and answer the questions by circling in the letter of the correct answer. Answer question 21 by filling in the blanks with your response.

You have 40 minutes to complete this section.

Inside a Baseball

Have you ever wondered what is inside a major-league baseball? Most people would not ruin a perfectly good ball to find out, but sometimes a ball comes apart from being used in a lot of games and practices. So if this should happen, and if you take it apart, here is what you will find. First you will remove the white cover. You will see that it is cut into two figure-8 shapes. They are made of cowhide. Each pattern covers half the finished baseball.

Go On

You will find that the cover has been stitched onto the ball with 88 inches of waxed red thread. The 108 stitches have been done by hand, because no one has been able to invent a machine that can do it. It takes an experienced worker about 14 minutes to stitch one ball.

Once the cover is off, you would see what looks like a large ball of tightly wrapped yarn. That is exactly what it is.

Next you will unwrap a layer of 150 yards of cotton finishing yarn. It is used to protect the woolen yarn underneath and hold it in place. You would then find 53 yards of gray wool, 45 yards of white wool, and 121 yards of gray wool—a total of 369 yards. If unrolled it would be longer than three football fields plus the end zones.

Once you have unwrapped all the yarn, you will find a cork center. It is covered with two layers of rubber. This center is called a *pill*. The yarn is wrapped so tightly around the pill that the finished ball, including its cover, is only nine inches around. It weighs a little more than five ounces. Baseballs must be inspected and approved for use in major-league games. Once in a game, they will be used for only about seven pitches. That's why the major leagues use more than 900,000 baseballs in a season.

Go On

Questions

1. According to the article, in what order will you find the yarn as you unwrap the ball?

   A. cotton finishing yarn, gray wool, white wool, gray wool

   B. cotton finishing yarn, white wool, gray wool, gray wool

   C. gray wool, cotton finishing yarn, white wool, gray wool

   D. gray wool, white wool, gray wool, cotton finishing yarn

2. The author **most likely** uses football fields as an example of the length of the yarn

   A. to give people a way to "see" how long the yarn is

   B. to explain how tightly the yarn is wrapped

   C. to interest football fans in the article

   D. to make the article more interesting

3. The author's purpose in writing this article is probably to

   A. encourage people to play baseball

   B. interest people in making baseballs

   C. inform people about baseballs

   D. advertise baseballs for sale

Go On

4. Why does the author arrange the details in the order he does?

A. That is the order used when putting a ball together.

B. That is the order of importance of the materials.

C. That is the order of the weight of the materials.

D. That is the order in which you find the parts when unwrapping a ball.

An Interesting Creature of the Sea

Flatback, leatherback, Kemp's ridley, green, olive ridley, hawksbill, loggerhead. These are all types of sea turtles. This very interesting creature is found in all the world's oceans except the Arctic Ocean.

Sea turtles have an amazing sense of time and location. Sea turtles live mostly at sea, but when females reach about 30, they return to land to nest and lay eggs. They are able to use the earth's magnetic field to navigate. They usually come to the same beach where they hatched.

Go On

The females dig a hole and lay from 70 to 190 eggs in it. Then they cover up the hole and return to the water. About two months later, the baby turtles hatch and crawl into the sea, where they float with the currents. Eventually they are able to swim and make their own way in the ocean.

Sea turtles are older than dinosaurs, but modern predators are a serious threat. They can live for more than 150 years. Because of poaching and egg hunting, the population of some sea turtles has declined from many thousands to just a few hundred. Illegal hunters kill them for their meat and their shells are used for many things. They are accidentally caught in fishing nets. Pollution is another danger.

Many groups are trying to change that. People realize the importance of sea turtles, as a natural wonder and as a tourist attraction. People are attracted to areas where the turtles come ashore. It gives them a chance to watch a natural wonder in person. It also provides money for the towns nearby.

People at places like the Mexican Center for the Turtle, near Escobilla Beach, work to protect turtles. Police patrol beaches to keep hunters away. Laws are being passed to protect the turtles from pollution. Other laws make it illegal to sell products made from turtle shells as souvenirs.

The work is hard and takes a long time. It is hoped that eventually, turtles will receive the protection they need and continue to be a valuable source of knowledge instead of food and souvenirs.

Go On

Questions

5. Which is NOT a type of sea turtle?

   A. olive ridley

   B. loggerhead

   C. lumberjack

   D. leatherback

6. As it is used in the last line of paragraph 2, the word *navigate* means

   A. hunt for food

   B. find their way

   C. lay their eggs

   D. hide from hunters

7. The author's purpose in writing this passage is **most likely**

   A. to amuse readers

   B. to entertain readers

   C. to inform readers

   D. to scare readers

8. According to the passage, a major reason for people to help sea turtles is that

   A. turtles have lived longer than dinosaurs

   B. turtles are good navigators

   C. turtles are a natural wonder

   D. turtles provide food for tourists

Go On

What It's All About

How'd I get here?
I ask myself a lot,
when I'm thinking about
things I could have done
with my life.

If I could have hit a curve,
for example,
and been a little taller,
and a step faster,
I could have been playin' ball on TV
and making the big money.

Or if I had hung in there
with law school,
I could have been a judge by now
or a senator,
or at least a partner in a firm,
and making the big money.

Go On

But instead I walked
into a school when I needed a job,
and once I caught on,
I could have been a principal,
or maybe even a superintendent,
and making the big money.

But I'm in a classroom
with a hundred and twenty kids
passing through every day,
trying to give them something that's
not about making the big money.

It's about when a conversation begins:
I had this teacher once . . .

Questions

9. The poet asks, "How'd I get here?" What does he mean by *here*?

   A. the town where he works

   B. the town where he lives

   C. the job that he has

   D. the job that he wants

10. According to the poem, some people think that it's important to

    A. make a lot of money

    B. wonder about your life

    C. be a professional athlete

    D. be good at many things

Go On

11. According to the poet, what is more important than making money?

    A. nothing

    B. being happy

    C. being healthy

    D. being a good teacher

12. If a conversation begins with *I had this teacher once,* it is **most likely** that the person

    A. liked the teacher

    B. didn't like the teacher

    C. can't remember the teacher

    D. avoided the teacher

Gone, but Not Forgotten

In 1930, Pluto was discovered. An astronomer named Clyde Tombaugh discovered it. It was declared to be the ninth planet in our solar system. Ever since it was

Go On

discovered, there has been an argument about whether or not Pluto is really a planet.

There are rules for being a planet. It must be an object that orbits the sun. It must be large enough to have become round because of its own gravity. Also, a planet has to "dominate the neighborhood" around its orbit.

Pluto is OK on the first two, but apparently it doesn't "dominate its neighborhood."

To dominate its neighborhood, a planet has to be sort of a bully. It has to clear out asteroids, comets, and other objects that might want to share its space. Pluto isn't big enough or strong enough to do this. So, Pluto's orbit is not very orderly. Sometimes it even overlaps Neptune's.

Recently, scientists met to decide Pluto's fate. The International Astronomical Union voted. Because it doesn't meet their standards, Pluto is no longer considered a planet.

In the end, the astronomers decided that only Mercury, Venus, Earth, Mars, Jupiter, Saturn, Uranus, and Neptune fit the definition of "classical planets."

But, what about Pluto? It has been reclassified a "dwarf planet." That makes it a little lower in status, but still famous.

Go On

Questions

13. One of the reasons that Pluto is no longer a planet is that it

    A. was unpopular

    B. was too hot

    C. was too "weak"

    D. was too cold

14. The decision to remove Pluto from the list of planets was made by

    A. astrologers

    B. meteorologists

    C. physicists

    D. astronomers

15. As used in the passage, the word *orbit* means

    A. size

    B. weight

    C. path

    D. mass

16. To be a "classical planet" a celestial body must

    A. have its own moon

    B. orbit around the moon

    C. be round

    D. be a bully

Go On

A Record-Setting Performance

Jason McElwain was the 17-year-old basketball team manager at Greece Athena High School, near Rochester, NY.

Jason has a condition known as autism. Autism can make it hard for people to learn and to deal with other people socially. This kept him from making the varsity basketball team. He volunteered to be the team's manager so that he could be involved in the sport he loves.

As manager, Jason has to be a jack-of-all-trades. He is responsible for such things as keeping track of equipment, helping the players and coaches at practices, and even keeping score. He never misses practices. He sits on the bench at games wearing a white shirt, dress trousers, and a black necktie. "He is happy to do it," Coach Jack

Go On

Johnson said. "He is such a great help and is well liked by everyone on the team."

Because of Jason's dedication and support of the team, Coach Johnson decided to let him suit up for the team's final regular-season game. It was thought that he might even get a chance to play. "J-Mac," as he is known, got his chance when Athena took a big lead with about four minutes left in the game.

Jason entered the game to loud, enthusiastic cheering from the home crowd. His teammates made sure he got the ball and a chance to shoot. Things didn't start off too well.

"My first shot was an air ball [missing the hoop] by a lot, then I missed a layup," he said. What happened next seems like a dream.

Jason's next shot, from three-point range, swished through the net. The crowd screamed with delight.

The next time Athena had the ball, his teammates made sure he shot again—*swish*.

With the crowd and his teammates screaming encouragement, whenever Greece had the ball, it went to Jason to shoot it. Again and again, *swish*. By the time the game ended, he had tied the team record for three-point baskets. He had scored 20 points in just four minutes on the court. He could have broken the record, but a possible seventh three-pointer didn't count because his foot was on the line. It counted as two points.

When the final buzzer sounded, delirious fans mobbed him. His teammates carried him off the court on their shoulders, a sign of respect for the hero of a game.

Go On

Jason had his own thoughts on his big moment. "I was really hotter than a pistol. I ended my career on the right note."

The story does not end there. Jason's exploits, sensational for any basketball player, but more noteworthy because of his autistic condition, became national news immediately. National networks showed films of his performance. He was not only on their sports programs, but also on the main part of their news show.

More important than the points he scored, Jason's heroics are an example of overcoming difficulties to reach a goal.

Because of his autism, Jason didn't talk until he was about five, and had difficulty in school because of his lack of social skills. He discovered basketball, which is a game that he could practice by himself, shooting shot after shot, day after day. Basketball was more than a hobby; it was a way for Jason to channel his energy into something positive.

Despite all the attention he has received, Jason's immediate goal was to be back at his manager's job, in his white shirt and tie, "trying to win a sectional title for the team."

Questions

17. Autism made it hard for Jason to make the team because

    A. it makes it hard to jump very high

    B. it makes it hard to get along with people

    C. it makes him get tired more easily

    D. it makes him unable to hear the coach

Go On

18. According to this passage a "jack-of-all-trades" is someone who

    A. is good at basketball

    B. is good at coaching

    C. is good at school

    D. is good at many things

19. Coach Johnson let Jason suit up and play because Jason was

    A. popular with the fans

    B. a really good player

    C. dedicated and hardworking

    D. the best manager ever

20. The author's main purpose in writing this article was most likely to

    A. tell about an amazing accomplishment

    B. give information about basketball

    C. explain what *autism* means

    D. tell about a good basketball team

21. Using details from the passage, explain why Jason's accomplishment was so amazing.

    _____

    _____

    _____

    _____

Go On

PART 2—LISTENING SECTION

On this part of the test you will listen to an article that will be read to you twice. During the first reading you should just listen carefully. During the second reading you should listen and take notes. You will use these notes to answer questions 22–26.

For questions 22–25, circle the correct answer. For question 26, write your response in the space provided. You may use your notes to answer the questions.

After the second reading, you will have 10 minutes to complete this part of the test.

Do not turn the page until you are told to do so.

NOTES:

Go On

STOP! Please have a teacher or parent read the following listening passage.

Go On

LISTENING PASSAGE FOR PRACTICE TEST ONE

Oak Island – Trick or Treat?

One day, in 1795, a boy named Daniel McGinnis rowed his boat to Oak Island in Nova Scotia. While exploring, he found something interesting. It looked like a spot where someone had filled in a hole. The next day, Daniel and two of his friends, John Smith and Anthony Vaughan dug in that spot to see if something was buried there.

Just below the surface they found a layer of stones. Under the stones was a round clay pit. Farther down they found a platform of oak logs. They moved the logs and found more clay. They kept digging and found more logs. Finally, they gave up and went home.

People in the area had thought that the famous pirate, Captain Kidd, might have buried some of his treasure in that area. As soon as people heard about the boys' adventure, they thought that Oak Island might be the place.

McGinnis and his two friends continued to try to find what might be down there. Because of the rumors of fabulous treasure, serious digging was begun about 1802.

Go On

A man named Simeon Lynds visited the money pit that year. He formed a company and provided money to excavate the pit.

They cleaned out the original pit which was 30 feet deep. They found something every ten feet. They found more stone and more logs all the way down to about 90 feet. There, they found a flat stone, three feet long and one foot wide, with strange letters and figures cut into it. They were unable to figure it out.

Once they passed that level, they were digging in soft mud. Then, something exciting happened. They reached a wooden barrier that they thought must be a treasure vault. Excited by their find, they quit for the day, knowing that the next day they would be rich.

When they returned the next day, they found the pit flooded with 60 feet of water. Their attempts to bail out the water failed. As the water was removed, more poured in. They tried digging a new shaft, but it flooded too. Their attempts to stop the water flow with dams failed and the search was abandoned for over 40 years.

In 1849, a new group of treasure hunters made an attempt. These diggers discovered a clever system that someone had put in place to protect the treasure. Drains from a nearby cove allowed seawater to flow into the mysterious pit. Engineers failed to solve the problem and the effort was abandoned in 1851.

The next attempt in 1861 failed and an exploding boiler pump killed one of the diggers. By 1864, this group of treasure hunters was also out of money.

Go On

Many more people tried and they all failed. No matter what they tried, water continued to flood the pit. Even after they blocked one source, water still flooded in.

Eventually drillers managed to drill down to 150 feet. They discovered what they thought might be treasure chests and recovered metal pieces and chain links – but no treasure. The pit continued to flood and the chests and metal objects were lost.

People continued to try and continued to fail. In 1959, four people were killed in one day in an accident in the pit. In 1965, huge mining machines were brought in. They were unsuccessful. In 1971, a TV camera was lowered 260 feet into the pit. All it showed was a blurry view of what they thought was a severed human hand. It was never seen again.

The last major attempt to solve the mystery and become rich was in 1995, 200 years after Daniel and his friends started digging. Again, the result was failure and more wasted money.

Today, people continue to plan ways to find the treasure, even though no one really knows if there is any.

Listening Passage Questions

22. Some people thought that the Money Pit contained
    A. Blackbeard's treasure
    B. Captain Kidd's treasure
    C. Daniel McGinness's treasure
    D. French Army treasure

Go On

23. When Daniel and his friends started digging, they found several layers of

    A. treasure

    B. water

    C. logs

    D. newspaper

24. Whoever built the pit designed it so that when diggers reached a certain level, it would fill up with

    A. stones

    B. clay

    C. gravel

    D. water

25. The place on Oak Island known as "The Money Pit" is called that because

    A. so much money has been spent trying to find its treasure

    B. so much treasure has been found there

    C. that is what Captain Kidd called it

    D. it was called that by the early settlers of Oak Island

26. Using at least three details from the story, explain why the mystery has never been solved.

_____

_____

_____

Go On

PART 3—EDITING

NOTE: On the actual test, students will have a chance to practice an editing passage here. Since you have already practiced the editing, it is omitted here.

✳✳✳

27. A student wrote this report about a respected person. You have ten minutes to find and correct the mistakes in this passage.

Perfect Attendance

Many students have perfect attendance, they go to school every day, even if they are sick. Some even have perfect attendance for their hole school career. That is very unusual.

A man named Cal Ripken Jr had perfect attendance too. His perfect attendance set a major-league baseball record. He had perfect attendance for more than 16 years as a

Go On

PRACTICE TEST TWO

PART 1—READING COMPREHENSION

Read the following passages and answer the questions by circling in the letter of the correct answer. Answer question 21 by filling in the blanks with your response.

You have 40 minutes to complete this section.

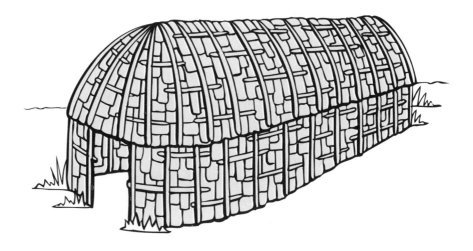

Native New Yorkers

The Iroquois League or Haudenosaunee are made up of six different tribes—the Onondaga, Cayuga, Oneida, Mohawk, Seneca, and Tuscarora. The center of the original Iroquois Confederacy was in New York. It was near where Syracuse is today. This was the home of the Onondaga tribe. Onondaga Lake is one of their most sacred areas.

Go On

Five tribes first made up the Iroquois. They were originally enemies. In the 1600s, they joined together to protect against invasion by other tribes and Europeans.

The name Iroquois may have come from an enemy tribe, the Algonquians. The Algonquians called them "Iroqu," which means rattlesnakes. The French who came to North America then called them Iroquois.

In the early 1700s the Tuscaroras joined them. Then they became known as the Six Nations. They took the name Haudenosaunee. It means "People of the Longhouse." A longhouse is just as the name suggests, a long house. They might be as long as 150 feet. They were made of wooden poles covered with tree bark. The longhouses made up a village. The village was usually surrounded by a stockade—a tall wooden fence.

Villages were made up of family groups called clans. The members of the same clan would live together in a longhouse. Clans were named for animals. A carved figure of that animal would hang over the door of their longhouse.

The Haudenosaunee have nine clans: Bear, Beaver, Deer, Eel, Hawk, Heron, Snipe, Turtle, and Wolf. A clan is a group of families who are related. A woman, known as the clan mother, leads them.

The clan mother was very powerful. She was in charge of choosing the clan's chiefs. She could remove a chief if she felt he was not a good leader.

The Haudenosaunee were mostly farmers. Their crops were very important. The men cleared the land. The women planted the crops. All the women of the clan

Go On

managed the land and crops. The women were mostly in charge of running the village.

Men were hunters and fishermen. They protected the villages and provided meat for the clan. They also traded with other tribes for goods they needed.

The adults were all responsible for educating the children. The children learned to do the things their parents did by helping the adults. This way, the tribal ways were passed from generation to generation.

The Haudenosaunee had one of the earliest democratic governments. Villages had their own leaders. Each tribe had a council. Clan mothers chose members of this council. The tribal council was in charge of making laws for the tribe. The tribal council also chose members of the Grand Council. Following the Great Law of the Iroquois League, the Grand Council met in late summer or early fall at Onondaga. The council made sure the league's laws were followed.

Today, the Iroquois live near the Great Lakes in Wisconsin, Pennsylvania, and New York. Some live in Oklahoma. Many also live in Canada, in the provinces of Ontario and Quebec. They number about 70,000.

Questions

1. The traditional name *Haudenosaunee* means
   A. People of the Longhouse
   B. People of the Villages
   C. People of Syracuse
   D. People of the Three Sisters

Go On

2. Which tribe was an enemy of the Iroquois?

   A. Oneida

   B. Seneca

   C. Algonquian

   D. Onondaga

3. The most powerful person in each clan was the

   A. clan chief

   B. council leader

   C. clan mother

   D. clan president

4. As it is used in the passage, the word *council* most nearly means

   A. a decision-making group

   B. a form of government

   C. the leader of a tribe

   D. the leader of a clan

5. The Haudenosaunee had a democratic government because

   A. the chief was a democrat

   B. a woman was the clan leader

   C. decisions were made by one person

   D. decisions were made by many people

Go On

Time

What is "time"? The actual dictionary definition is very complicated. We can think of time as a way of measuring how long it takes for something to happen. We think of it as a way of knowing when to be somewhere like school or an appointment. We think of it as a way to know when a game will be over. These are all examples of how time is important. But, without a way to measure it, it would be useless.

Thousands of years ago nobody needed to know about time. People would be awake when it was light, asleep when it was dark. There were no appointments or schedules. There were no games. People only needed to know when to plant crops or migrate to a warmer climate. They figured these things out by what the weather was like or where the sun or moon was in the sky.

Eventually people needed to divide the periods of light and dark. Possibly that was so they would know when to hold religious services. The Romans might need to know how long the senate should meet. People might need to know when to gather for meals.

Go On

The first clocks used the sun. A stick driven into the ground would produce a shadow. The shadow would move as the sun moved. This led to the earliest clocks, the sundials. They were first used about 5,500 years ago. A sundial had markings to indicate the time as the shadow fell on them. Of course, the problem with the sundial is that without sun, it was useless. So, it could not be used at night, indoors, or on cloudy days.

About 3,400 years ago, water clocks were invented in Egypt. They were made of two bowls filled with water. One was above the other. Water ran down from the higher one to the lower one through a tube. Marks on them showed how the water level changed. This was the time marking. Water clocks were better than sundials. They were more accurate. They could be used indoors and at night.

Another early clock was the sand clock or hourglass. They measured time by the flow of sand from the top to the bottom. They also could be used indoors and at night. Now, time itself could be more useful.

The Egyptians were probably the people who divided the day into 24 hours of equal length. This meant that it didn't matter whether it was day or night, light or dark. Now the time could be measured much more accurately.

Still, there needed to be better and more accurate clocks. People were depending more on knowing what time it was wherever they were. About 1655 a man named Christian Huygens invented a clock operated by a pendulum. A pendulum is a stick with a weight on the end. The weight makes it swing back and forth. As it swings, it turns a wheel with teeth. The turning wheel turns the hour and minute hands on the clock. It was powered by weights that turned gears as they moved down a chain.

Go On

A problem with a pendulum clock was that it would not work at sea. Sailors needed to know the time to know their location. So, the next great invention was very important to them.

A contest was held to inspire people to invent such a clock. John Harrison, a carpenter, was the winner of the contest. It took him more than thirty years to produce the winner. In it, a tightly wound spring moved the clock's hands as it uncoiled. That way they were able to determine their location more accurately.

The spring clock made modern wristwatches possible. Now everyone was able to know the exact time wherever they were.

Today, the quartz clock is the most accurate available to the average person. Quartz is a type of crystal. If electricity is applied, it vibrates and moves the clock's hands. Even though they were invented in 1920, they are still the most reliable today.

Today, scientists use atomic clocks that are so accurate they might be off by only about a second every 300 million years. For them, such incredible accuracy is important. For the average person, a nice, accurate wristwatch is enough to keep us on schedule so that we can arrive where we need to be precisely on time.

Questions

6. The first actual clocks told time by using

    A. candles

    B. sunlight

    C. moonlight

    D. water

Go On

7. According to the article, the most accurate clocks among the following is the

   A. sundial

   B. water clock

   C. pendulum clock

   D. spring clock

8. A problem with the sundial was that

   A. it needed batteries to work

   B. there were no time zones

   C. it did not work indoors

   D. it was hard to wind

9. In the last paragraph, the word *precisely* most nearly means

   A. slowly

   B. exactly

   C. quickly

   D. clearly

Go On

Jeans

Look around your classroom. What kind of pants are most of the kids wearing? Probably the answer is jeans. Go to the mall. The answer would be the same. Even in businesses and other workplaces you will find people wearing jeans. People wear jeans as a fashion item with expensive sweaters and sport coats. Movie stars, athletes, doctors, lawyers, and professors—all can be found wearing jeans at some time.

The first "waist-overalls" were created about 1873 in Reno, Nevada. A tailor named Jacob Davis sewed them together. Originally, blue jeans were work pants, designed for miners to wear. Jeans were tough, made of a French invention, material called denim. They were sewn together with tough thread. Metal fasteners called rivets were added to the pants to help them hold up under the stress

Go On

of hard work. Rivets are the same fasteners used in the construction of skyscrapers and airplanes.

Eventually, Davis became partners with a man named Levi Strauss. The pants were soon known by people who bought them as "Levi's." In 1880, a pair of Levi overalls cost $1.25.

They haven't changed much since they were invented. Belt loops were added in the 1920s because workers had stopped wearing suspenders to hold up their pants. Some Levi's also featured loops to hold tools, such as hammers or paintbrushes.

In the 1950s, teenagers had taken to wearing jeans as a sign of rebellion against the way they were "supposed" to dress. By the 1960s, the jeans had become bell-bottomed "hippie" clothing, but by the '70s they were a fashion item worn by adults as well as kids.

Now, jeans are the universal look. They are sold all over the world by hundreds of companies. They are sold frayed and worn and faded. Some have holes in them as if they were worn out. High fashion jeans can cost as much as five hundred dollars. They are still even worn by the people they were invented for, miners.

Questions

10. The first jeans were made to be worn by

    A. farmers

    B. miners

    C. hippies

    D. sailors

Go On

11. As used in the last paragraph, the expression *universal look* most closely means

   A. worn by miners

   B. worn by professors

   C. worn by athletes

   D. worn by everyone

12. Belt loops were added to jeans in the

   A. 1870s

   B. 1920s

   C. 1960s

   D. 1980s

13. An important part of the original success of jeans was

   A. adding rivets at stress points to make them stronger

   B. prewashing the finished pants to make them fade

   C. changing the name to jeans from overalls

   D. making them fashionable to wear to parties

Go On

America's Doorway

On January 1, 1892, the door to America swung open. From then until 1954, more than 12 million immigrants passed through it.

That doorway was Ellis Island in New York Harbor. It is close to the Statue of Liberty. Seventy percent of all immigrants at the time were processed there. The ancestors of more than 40 percent of Americans arrived here by way of Ellis Island.

The process for entering the United States was partly based on status. Passengers who could afford to travel with first- and second-class tickets were not considered to be a risk. When the ships docked at piers on the Hudson River, the first- and second-class passengers could leave and pass through Customs. Then they were free to enter the United States.

Go On

The situation was very different for "steerage" or third-class passengers. They traveled to America in crowded and unsanitary conditions. They slept near the bottom of their ships. After the ships docked, they were transported to Ellis Island, where everyone would undergo a medical and legal inspection.

First they had to pass a physical examination. Some with health problems or diseases such as measles were sent home. About 2 percent were sent back. Others were held in the island's hospital facilities for long periods of time. They were asked questions including name, occupation, and the amount of money they carried with them. Criminals and other risky people were also sent back.

The Ellis Island inspection process would last approximately three to five hours. The inspections took place in the Registry Room (or Great Hall). Doctors would briefly scan every immigrant for obvious physical ailments. This happened very quickly. A doctor could identify numerous medical conditions just by glancing at an immigrant. These were called "six-second physicals." If they were healthy, their papers were checked. If they were in order, people were then allowed to leave. They were now in America.

Eventually, immigration into America slowed down. By 1954, Ellis Island was no longer needed as a processing center.

In 1965, President Lyndon Johnson declared Ellis Island part of the Statue of Liberty National Monument. From 1976 to 1984 the main building was open to the public. Starting in 1984, Ellis Island underwent a major restoration. The $160 million project was the largest historic restoration in U.S. history. The money was raised by donations made by the American people. Now, every

Go On

year nearly 2 million people visit this important historical site.

Questions

14. As used in the passage, the word *immigrants* most nearly means
    A. wealthy travelers by ship
    B. people entering a country
    C. people leaving a country
    D. someone with no home

15. Steerage passengers were probably
    A. not healthy
    B. not wealthy
    C. not wise
    D. not popular

16. According to the passage a person would most likely be allowed into America if he or she
    A. had the measles
    B. had been in prison
    C. had a lot of money
    D. had no job skills

17. According to the passage, the U.S. government probably spent so much money to restore Ellis Island because
    A. they might need to use it again
    B. it would attract tourists
    C. it is near the Statue of Liberty
    D. it is important to many Americans

Go On

Nothing to Write About

Sara Ciarlei

I have a poem due Monday.
It's Sunday.
I feel stuck—frustrated, brain dead.

I have nothing to write about.
That's my problem.
To write a poem you need ideas.

I look around me to give me the answer,
I see nothing.
Nobody here to help me.
Alone.

Why is it I'm creative,
but I can't write
stupid lines on paper?

I tell myself I'm poetic, I can do it.
But, this empty paper stares back at me,
Telling me I can't.
I'm starting to believe it.

Go On

Maybe if I open a poetry book,
copy a few lines,
no one would find out . . . but I'd know.

Oh, I wish I could
just write a stupid poem!

Questions

18. The writer of this poem is most likely

   A. a student

   B. a teacher

   C. a poet

   D. a parent

19. The irony in this poem is that

   A. she wrote a poem about how she couldn't write one

   B. she was afraid that she would get a bad grade and didn't

   C. she knew that she would be able to do it but couldn't

   D. she knew that it didn't matter if she did it, so she didn't

20. According to the poem, it is most likely that she didn't copy a poem by someone else because

   A. she couldn't find one

   B. she didn't have time

   C. she knew it was wrong

   D. she lost her notebook

Go On

21. Use details from the poem to tell why Sara was having problems writing a poem.

_____

_____

_____

_____

PART 2—LISTENING SECTION

On this part of the test you will listen to an article that will be read to you twice. During the first reading you should just listen carefully. During the second reading you should listen and take notes. You will use these notes to answer questions 22–26.

For questions 22–25, circle the correct answer. For question 26, write your response in the space provided. You may use your notes to answer the questions.

After the second reading, you will have 10 minutes to complete this part of the test.

Do not turn the page until you are told to do so.

NOTES:

Go On

STOP! Please have a teacher or parent read the following listening passage.

Go On

LISTENING PASSAGE FOR PRACTICE TEST TWO

John Glenn—No Time Limit for a Hero

On October 29, 1998, on board the space shuttle *Discovery,* a man named John Glenn lifted off for his second space flight. Going into space for a second time was not so unusual. What was unusual was that his first space flight had been in 1962. Now, thirty-six years later, he was the oldest person ever to fly in space. John Glenn was 77-years-old.

On his previous flight aboard *Friendship 7* he had been the first American astronaut to orbit Earth. He had been only the third American ever to fly in space.

Go On

Another unusual fact is that at the time of his *Discovery* flight, John Glenn was also a United States Senator from Ohio.

In 1964, Glenn had resigned from the space program. It was rumored that President John F. Kennedy had considered John Glenn to be such an important national hero that he should not be risked on another space mission. In 1965, Glenn retired as a Colonel from the United States Marine Corps.

Eventually, he entered politics. In 1968, he ran for a seat in the United States Senate. He was defeated in that election but won in 1974. For the next 24 years, John Glenn served as a senator from the state of Ohio.

While serving in the Senate, he was a member of the Senate Special Committee on Aging. He became aware that many older people suffer from some of the same problems as astronauts in space. Sleep problems, bone and muscle weakness, and dizziness occur in both. Glenn said that he thought that by sending an older person into space, a lot could be learned that might help older people.

Glenn felt that the best person for the job was – John Glenn.

He approached NASA with his idea, and on January 15, 1997, he received great news. The mission was "go" (NASA talk for OK) if he could complete a flight physical and undergo the same training as the rest of the crew. He accepted immediately.

He passed the physical at the Johnson Space Center easily because he had stayed in good physical shape. He completed the training with his fellow astronauts and blasted off on the nine-day mission.

Go On

Once in space, he wore electronic sensors to measure his sleep patterns and brain waves. Scientists hoped to learn more about the aging process by studying the results of Glenn's tests. The mission's captain reported that "John has a smile on his face, and it goes from one ear to the other." There were a number of tasks for him to perform during the mission. Despite being a United States Senator, he worked right along with the rest of the crew. For the time being, he was "just" an astronaut.

Following their safe return, Glenn and his crewmates were honored with a ticker tape parade down the Canyon of Heroes in New York City. For Glenn, it was his second such honor, thirty-six years after he had first been recognized as one of America's great heroes. Coincidentally, the son of the man who had driven him in the parade in 1962 drove the car.

When asked what he had learned on the mission, he said, "I've noticed that maybe because of all this, people are seeing themselves in a way they haven't before. They're realizing that older people have the same ambitions, hopes, and dreams as anybody else. I say you should live life based on how you feel and not by the calendar."

Listening Passage Questions

22. When John Glenn first flew into space, the president was

A. William Clinton

B. George Bush

C. John F. Kennedy

D. George Clinton

Go On

23. John Glenn is probably most famous for being

    A. an astronaut

    B. a senator

    C. a marine

    D. a national hero

24. According to the passage, John Glenn would **best** be described as being

    A. frustrated

    B. adventurous

    C. excited

    D. intelligent

25. John Glenn first orbited Earth aboard a ship called

    A. *The John F. Kennedy*

    B. *Discovery*

    C. *Freedom 7*

    D. *Friendship 7*

26. Using details from the story, explain why John Glenn's two space flights were unusual.

_____

_____

_____

_____

Go On

PART 3—EDITING

Practice editing

NOTE: On the actual test, students will have a chance to practice an editing passage here. Since you have already practiced the editing, it is omitted here.

* *

27. A student wrote this report about the first men to drive a car across the United States. You have 10 minutes to find and correct the mistakes in this passage.

A Long, Long Ride

in 1903, H. Nelson Jackson and Sewall K. Crocker drove a car from California to New York. That would not be anything special today. However they were the first to ever do it.

Go On

In 1903 they did not have very good roads. A lot of them were dirt, they got very muddy they got stuck a lot. There were not many gas stations so they had to take a lot of gas with them

They drove a car called a Winton and took along a dog named bud. It took them 63 days to drive from San Francisco California to New York City.

ANSWERS AND EXPLANATIONS FOR PRACTICE TESTS 1 AND 2

PRACTICE TEST ONE: CORRECT RESPONSES

READING COMPREHENSION

Inside a Baseball

1. According to the article, in what order will you find the yarn as you unwrap the ball?

    A. cotton finishing yarn, gray wool, white wool, gray wool

    ■ There is a **SEQUENCE**. In paragraph 4, the order of unwrapping is given. First you will unwrap a layer of 150 yards of cotton finishing yarn used to protect the woolen yarn underneath and hold it in place. You would then find 53 yards of gray wool, 45 yards of white wool, and another 121 yards of gray wool.

2. The author most likely uses football fields as an example of the length of the yarn

    A. to give people a way to "see" how long the yarn is

■ Your **INFERENCE** would be based on experience. People can "see" a football field in their mind and compare that with the length of the yarn that would be unrolled.

3. The author's purpose in writing this article is probably to

    C. inform people about baseballs

    ■ The passage contains **DETAILS** (information) about what is inside a baseball. The use of **DETAILS** throughout the whole passage is usually to inform.

4. Why does the author arrange the details in the order he does?

    D. That is the order in which you find the parts when unwrapping a ball.

    ■ The author uses a logical **SEQUENCE** to help the reader understand the way the ball is made and visualize what would happen during the unwrapping.

An Interesting Creature of the Sea

5. Which is NOT a type of sea turtle?

    C. lumberjack

    ■ This is **FACT-BASED.** All the other types of sea turtle are listed.

6. As it is used in the last line of paragraph 2, the word *navigate* means

    B. find their way

    ■ By using the **CONTEXT CLUES**, you know that the turtles are traveling to specific beaches. They use the earth's magnetic field to do that, so if they are navigating, they are finding their way.

7. The author's purpose in writing this passage is most likely

    C. to inform readers

▪ The passage is mostly DETAILS (information) about sea turtles. Our INFERENCE would be that he is using them because he wants to inform (tell) the readers about sea turtles.

8. According to the passage, a major reason for people to help sea turtles is that

    C. turtles are a natural wonder

▪ DETAILS in the passage say that people appreciate the turtle as a natural wonder, and because of that, there are other benefits to the Mexican people. Protecting the turtles helps to protect those benefits.

What It's All About

9. The poet asks, "How'd I get here?" What does he mean by *here*?

    C. the job that he has

▪ This is an INFERENCE based on the fact that he is talking about jobs he could have had and how they compare with the job that he has now.

10. According to the poem, some people think that it's important to

    A. make a lot of money

▪ He said that he could have "been making the big money" in other jobs. He IMPLIES (suggests) that that might be why people have those jobs.

11. According to the poet, what is more important than making money?

    D. being a good teacher

▪ He **IMPLIES** that his job is about something other than how much money someone could make and that being a good teacher is more important to him.

12. If a conversation begins with *I had this teacher once,* it is **most likely** that the person

A. liked the teacher

▪ The **INFERENCE** you make from your own experience is that we all tend to talk more about people we like than those we don't. If we are going to tell a story about a teacher, it is probably a teacher we liked.

Gone, but Not Forgotten

13. One of the reasons that Pluto is no longer a planet is that it

C. was too "weak"

▪ This is **FACT-BASED.** It says that to be a planet, a celestial body has to be able to clear out asteroids, comets, and other objects that might want to share its space. Pluto isn't big enough or strong enough to do this.

14. The decision to remove Pluto from the list of planets was made by

D. astronomers

▪ This is also **FACT- BASED.** The answer is found in the statement "In the end, the astronomers decided."

15. As used in the passage, the word *orbit* means

C. path

▪ **VOCABULARY/CONTEXT.** We know that planets must orbit the sun. We also know that planets move in a path around the sun, so "path" would be the answer.

16. To be a "classical planet" a celestial body must

    C. be round

▪ This is FACT- BASED because it says that a planet "must be large enough to have become round because of its own gravity."

A Record-Setting Performance

17. Autism made it hard for Jason to make the team because

    B. it makes it hard to get along with people

▪ The INFERENCE you must make is that if it is hard to get along with people, it would be difficult to be part of a team.

18. According to this passage a "jack-of-all-trades" is someone who

    D. is good at many things

▪ You would have to make the INFERENCE that he is good at the many things that he does in order to have the job. "He is responsible for such things as keeping track of equipment, helping the players and coaches at practices, and even keeping score."

19. Coach Johnson let Jason suit up and play because Jason was

    C. dedicated and hardworking

▪ You would make the INFERENCE that the coach is giving Jason a reward for all his hard work and loyalty to the team.

20. The author's main purpose in writing this article was most likely to

    A. tell about an amazing accomplishment

    ▪ Even though the author talks about all the choices, the best choice would be because that is the MAIN IDEA of the passage.

Short Response

21. Using details from the passage, explain why Jason's accomplishment was so amazing.

Possible correct responses

- ▪ He had autism. It says in the passage that the condition "kept him from making the varsity basketball team."
- ▪ He was the team's manager, not a regular player. It took a special act by the coach to give him the chance to play.
- ▪ He had never played in a game before. Since he was not on the team, he would not have played, which would make it very difficult to be able to deal with the pressure of game situations.
- ▪ It's very difficult to make three-point shots. Making six of them, like he did, would be unusual even for professional basketball players.
- ▪ He played only four minutes in the game. Four minutes is a very short period of time in a basketball game, so it was unusual for him to get that many chances to shoot in such a short period of time.
- ▪ He tied the team record for three-point baskets. To tie a record is unusual, because records are the best accomplishments.

NOTE: Any other responses judged to satisfy the requirement can also be considered correct.

LISTENING COMPREHENSION

Oak Island – Trick or Treat?

22. Some people thought that the Money Pit contained

   B. Captain Kidd's treasure

   ▪ This is FACT-BASED/INFERENCE. It says in the passage that Captain Kidd, the famous pirate, was rumored to have buried some treasure somewhere off the coast of Nova Scotia. That might cause people to think it might be on Oak Island.

23. When Daniel and his friends started digging, they found several layers of

   C. logs

   ▪ This is FACT-BASED. The DETAILS of the passage describe what they found as they dug.

24. Whoever built the pit designed it so that when diggers reached a certain level, it would fill with

   D. water

   ▪ FACT-BASED. It says in the passage that "These diggers discovered a clever system that someone had put in place to protect the treasure. Drains from a nearby cove allowed seawater to flow into the mysterious pit."

25. The place on Oak Island known as "The Money Pit" is called that because

   A. so much money has been spent trying to find its treasure

   ▪ You can make an INFERENCE that the answer is **A** because a lot of money has been spent digging in the pit and no money has been found. Also, there is no proof that the other choices are correct.

26. Using at least three details from the story, explain wh the mystery has never been solved.

Possible Correct Responses

- Diggers found a platform of oak logs. They moved the logs and found more. They gave up and went home.
- They reached a wooden barrier that they thought must be a treasure vault. When they returned the next day, they found the pit flooded with 60 feet of water.
- Their attempts to bail out the water failed. As the water was removed, more poured in.
- They tried digging a new shaft, but it flooded too.
- Their attempts to stop the water flow with dams failed and the search was abandoned.
- Drains from a nearby cove allowed seawater to flow into the mysterious pit.
- Engineers failed to solve the problem and the effort was abandoned in 1851.
- By 1864 this group of treasure hunters was also ou of money.
- No matter what they tried, water continued to flood the pit.
- In 1965 huge mining machines were brought in. They were unsuccessful.

NOTE: Any other correct responses are also acceptable.

EDITING

Perfect Attendance

Many students have perfect <u>attendance, they</u> go to school every day, even if they are sick. Some even have perfect attendance for their <u>hole</u> school career. That is very unusual.

A man named Cal Ripken <u>Jr</u> had perfect attendance too. His perfect attendance set a major-league baseball record. He had perfect attendance for more than 16 years as a major-league baseball player. He played in <u>2632</u> consecutive games. That is 502 games more than Lou <u>Gehrigs</u> record that he <u>break</u>.

Correct Responses

Line 1: It is a run-on sentence that can be corrected in the following ways:

Many students have perfect attendance. They . . .

OR

Many students have perfect attendance; they . . .

Line 3: *Hole* is an incorrect word. It should read, "Some even have perfect attendance for their whole school career."

Line 5: A man named Cal Ripken Jr. had perfect attendance too. *Jr* requires a period after it since it is the abbreviation for *Junior.*

Line 8: 2,632 There must be a comma in numbers consisting of more than three digits.

Line 10: Gehrig's: This is a possessive. Gehrig owned the record.

Line 10: broke: This is the correct form of the past tense of *break.*

NOTE: Any correct change that does not create a new error is also acceptable.

PRACTICE TEST TWO: CORRECT RESPONSES

READING COMPREHENSION

Native New Yorkers

1. The traditional name *Haudenosaunee* means

    A. People of the Longhouse

    ▪ This is a FACT-BASED question. The DETAILS of the passage tell us that They took the name Haudenosaunee. It means "People of the Longhouse."

2. Which tribe was an enemy of the Iroquois?

    C. Algonquian

    ▪ This is a FACT-BASED question. The DETAILS of the passage tell us "The name Iroquois may have come from an enemy tribe, the Algonquians."

3. The most powerful person in each clan was the

    C. clan mother

    ▪ You can INFER this to be the correct answer. The clan mother is said to be "very powerful." She led her clan and had the authority to remove a chief if he did not do a good job.

4. As it is used in the passage, the word *council* most nearly means

    A. a decision-making group

    ▪ This is INFERENCE/FACT-BASED. Since "The tribal council was in charge of making laws for the tribe," they had to make decisions to do that.

5. The Haudenosaunee had a democratic government because

    D. decisions were made by many people

▪ This is **INFERENCE/FACT-BASED**. The passage gives several examples of the ways decisions and laws were made. All were done by a number of people or groups. From your studies, you know that that is how a democracy works.

Time

6. The first actual clocks told time by using

    B. sunlight

▪ This is a **FACT-BASED** question. According to the passage, "the first clocks used the sun."

7. According to the article, the most accurate clocks among the following is the

    D. spring clock

▪ This is a **FACT-BASED/INFERENCE** question. It says that "The spring clock made modern wrist-watches possible. Now everyone was able to know the exact time wherever they were." Each of the other clocks had a problem with its accuracy.

8. A problem with the sundial was that

    C. it did not work indoors

▪ This is a **FACT-BASED** question. The passage tells us that "without sun, it was useless. So, it could not be used at night, indoors, or on cloudy days."

9. In the last paragraph, the word *precisely* most nearly means

    B. exactly

■ This is a VOCABULARY/ CONTEXT CLUES question. The purpose of the article was to show how clocks had gone from not very accurate to being exceptionally accurate. So, the only word that makes sense when it is substituted for *precisely* is *exactly*.

Jeans

10. The first jeans were made to be worn by

     B. miners

     ■ This is FACT-BASED. The passage tells us that "blue jeans were work pants, designed for miners t wear."

11. As used in the last paragraph, the expression *universal look* most closely means

     D. worn by everyone

     ■ This is an INFERENCE question. A lot of people are said to wear jeans, so the word *universal* would best seem to relate to everyone.

12. Belt loops were added to jeans in the

     B. 1920s

     ■ This is a FACT-BASED question. The information is given in the passage.

13. An important part of the original success of jeans was

     A. adding rivets at stress points to make them stronger

     ■ You could make the INFERENCE that if the pants were worn by miners or others with hard jobs, it would be very important for them to be tough. Therefore, the workers would like the pants and keep buying them.

America's Doorway

14. As used in the passage, the word "immigrants" most nearly means

    B. people entering a country

    ▪ This is a VOCABULARY/INFERENCE question. Ellis Island was a place where people entered the country, so if immigrants arrived there, they would be people entering a country.

15. Steerage passengers were probably

    B. not wealthy

    ▪ This is an INFERENCE question. Since they were traveling in bad conditions, they likely could not afford better. Therefore, the answer not wealthy would be best.

16. According to the passage a person would most likely be allowed into America if he or she

    C. had a lot of money

    ▪ The question is FACT-BASED because it says that people with diseases like measles or those with criminal records could be sent back. Job skills are not mentioned. It says that it was easy for wealthy people (people with a lot of money) to get in.

17. According to the passage, the U.S. government probably spent so much money to restore Ellis Island because

    D. it is important to many Americans

    ▪ In the passage it says that 12 million Americans came through Ellis Island. It also says that 40 percent of Americans can trace their ancestry to those immigrants. The INFERENCE you should make is that because so many people are affected by Ellis

Island's place in history, it is important to many Americans.

Nothing to Write About

18. The writer of this poem is most likely

    A. a student

    ▪ This is an INFERENCE question. The poem is "due Monday," and your experience tells you that this is a common problem for students.

19. The irony in this poem is that

    A. she wrote a poem about how she couldn't write one

    ▪ The INFERENCE from your own experience is that it is ironic (the opposite of what you think should happen) that she was able to write a poem about being unable to write a poem.

20. According to the poem, it is most likely that she didn't copy a poem by someone else because

    C. she knew it was wrong.

    ▪ Your INFERENCE would be that she IMPLIES that even though "no one would know," she would know that it's wrong.

Short Response

21. Use details from the poem to tell why Sara was having problems writing a poem.

Possible acceptable responses - problems and reasons.

Pressure, deadline:

    ▪ poem due Monday
    ▪ it's Sunday

Frustration, lack of ideas:

- feels stuck – frustrated, brain dead
- nothing to write about – to write a poem you need ideas
- creative, but I can't write lines on paper

Lack of confidence:

- empty paper stares back at me – telling me I can't
- starting to believe it
- nobody here to help – alone

Temptation to copy:

- if I open a poetry book – copy a few lines
- no one would find out, but I'd know

NOTE: Any other correct responses are also acceptable.

LISTENING COMPREHENSION

John Glenn – No Time Limit for a Hero

22. When John Glenn first flew into space, the president was

C. John F. Kennedy

- This is a **FACT-BASED/INFERENCE** question. John F. Kennedy is the only president mentioned, and he called John Glenn a national hero and may have kept him from going into space again. He would have to have been president at that time.

23. John Glenn is probably most famous for being

A. an astronaut

- Your **INFERENCE** would be that even though all the other jobs are mentioned, the article is mostly about his being an astronaut.

24. According to the passage, John Glenn would best be described as being

   B. adventurous

   ▪ The article is mostly about his adventures in space, so he would be an adventurous person.

25. John Glenn first orbited Earth aboard a ship called

   D. *Friendship 7*

   ▪ This is a FACT-BASED question. In the passage it says that "he first flew into space on *Friendship 7*."

26. Using details from the story, explain why John Glenn' two space flights were unusual.

Possible correct responses:

FIRST FLIGHT – *Friendship 7*

   ▪ He was the first man to orbit the earth.
   ▪ He was chosen from among seven astronauts.
   ▪ They didn't know much about space flight.
   ▪ He had a parade to celebrate his achievement.
   ▪ The president called him a "national hero" and wouldn't let him go into space again.

NOTE: Any other correct responses are also acceptable.

SECOND FLIGHT – *Discovery*

   ▪ He was the oldest man to orbit the earth.
   ▪ He was 77.
   ▪ He was a U.S. Senator at the time.
   ▪ He rode in another parade to honor this mission.
   ▪ The son of the man who had driven him in the parade in 1962 drove him in 1998.

NOTE: Any other correct responses are also acceptable.

EDITING

A Long, Long Ride

in 1903, H. Nelson Jackson and Sewall K. Crocker drove a car from California to New York. That would not be anything special today. However they were the first to ever do it.

In 1903 they did not have very good roads. A lot of them were dirt, they got very muddy they got stuck a lot. There were not many gas stations so they had to take a lot of gas with them

They drove a car called a Winton and took along a dog named bud. It took them 63 days to drive from San Francisco California to New York City.

Correct Responses

Line 1: Capitalize In because it is the first word in a sentence.

Line 3: Place a comma between *However* and *they*.

Lines 5 and 6: This is a run-on sentence, and it is hard to tell what or who *they* refers to. It can be corrected in different ways:

> *A lot of them were dirt and they got very muddy. The men got stuck a lot.*

OR *A lot of them were dirt. They got very muddy. The men got stuck a lot.*

OR *A lot of the roads were dirt and got very muddy. They got stuck a lot.*

OR   Any other acceptable change.

Line 8: There must be a period after the word *them* at the end of the sentence.

Line 10: *Bud* should be capitalized because it is the name of their dog.

Lines 10 and 11: *San Francisco, California* should have a comma between the name of the city and state.

APPENDIX

Grade 5

Core Performance Indicators Common to All Four ELA Standards

Throughout grade 5, students demonstrate the following core performance indicators in the key ideas of reading, writing, listening, and speaking.

Reading	Writing
• Identify purpose of reading • Adjust reading rate according to purpose for reading • Use word recognition and context clues to read fluently • Determine the meaning of unfamiliar words by using context clues, a dictionary, or a glossary • Identify signal words, such as *finally* or *in addition*, that provide clues to organizational formats such as time order • Use knowledge of punctuation to assist in comprehension • Apply corrective strategies (e.g., rereading and discussion with teachers, peers, or	• Understand the purpose for writing; the purpose may be to explain, describe, narrate, persuade, or express feelings • Determine the intended audience before writing • Use tone and language appropriate for audience and purpose • Use prewriting activities (e.g., brainstorming, note taking, freewriting, outlining, and paragraphing) • Use the writing process (e.g., prewriting, drafting, revising, proofreading, and editing)

parents/caregivers) to assist in comprehension
- Read aloud, using inflection and intonation appropriate to text read and to audience
- Maintain a personal reading list to reflect reading goals and accomplishments

Listening

- Listen respectfully and responsively
- Identify own purpose for listening
- Recognize content-specific vocabulary or terminology
- Listen for unfamiliar words and learn their meaning

Speaking

- Respond respectfully
- Initiate communication with peers, teachers, and others in the school community
- Use language and grammar appropriate to purpose for speaking
- Use facial expressions and gestures that enhance communication
- Establish eye contact during presentations and group discussions
- Use audible voice and pacing appropriate to content and audience

- Use teacher conferences and peer review to revise written work
- Observe the rules of punctuation, capitalization, and spelling, such as
  - punctuation of compound sentences, friendly/business letters, simple dialogue, and exact words from sources (quotations); use italics/underlining for titles
  - capitalization of proper nouns such as key words in literary and/or book titles, languages, and historical events
  - spelling of commonly misspelled words, homonyms, and content-area vocabulary
- Use correct grammatical construction in
  - parts of speech such as nouns; adjectives and adverbs (comparative/superlative); pronouns (indefinite/nominative/objective); conjunctions (coordinating/subordinating); prepositions and prepositional phrases; and interjections
  - simple/compound/complex sentences, using correct subject-verb agreement, verb tense, punctuation, and pronouns with clear antecedents

• Use visual aids to support the presentation	• Use signal/transitional words (e.g., *in addition, for example, finally, as a result, similarly, and on the other hand*) to provide clues to organizational format • Use dictionaries, thesauruses, and style manuals • Use word processing skills

Grade 5 Reading

LITERACY COMPETENCIES	GRADE-SPECIFIC PERFORMANCE INDICATORS
The reading competencies common to all four ELA standards that students demonstrate during grade 5 are as follows:	The grade-specific performance indicators that grade 5 students demonstrate as they learn to read consist of the following:
Word Recognition	Standard 1: Students will read, write, listen, and speak for information and understanding.
• Use knowledge of a variety of decoding strategies, such as letter-sound correspondence, syllable patterns, decoding by analogy, word structure, use of syntactic (grammar) cues, and use of semantic (meaning) cues, to read unfamiliar words • Integrate sources of information to decode unfamiliar words and to cross-check, self-correcting when appropriate • Use word recognition skills and strategies, accurately and	• Locate and use school and public library resources, with some direction, to acquire information • Use tables of contents and indexes to locate information • Read to collect and interpret data, facts, and ideas from multiple sources • Read the steps in a procedure in order to accomplish a task such

automatically, when decoding unfamiliar words
- Recognize at sight a large body of high-frequency words and irregularly spelled content vocabulary

Background Knowledge and Vocabulary Development

- Learn grade-level vocabulary through both direct and indirect means
- Use word structure knowledge, such as roots, prefixes, and suffixes, to determine meaning
- Use prior knowledge and experience to understand ideas and vocabulary found in books
- Acquire new vocabulary by reading a variety of texts
- Use self-monitoring strategies to identify specific vocabulary that causes comprehension difficulties
- Determine the meaning of unfamiliar words by using context clues, dictionaries, glossaries, and other resources
- Use a thesaurus to identify synonyms and antonyms

Comprehension Strategies

- Read a variety of grade-level texts, for a variety of purposes, with understanding

as completing a science experiment
- Skim material to gain an overview of content or locate specific information
- Use text features, such as headings, captions, and titles, to understand and interpret informational texts
- Recognize organizational formats to assist in comprehension of informational texts
- Identify missing information and irrelevant information
- Distinguish between fact and opinion
- Identify information that is implied rather than stated
- Compare and contrast information on one topic from multiple sources
- Recognize how new information is related to prior knowledge or experience
- Identify main ideas and supporting details in informational texts to distinguish relevant and irrelevant information
- Make inferences and draw conclusions, on the basis of information from the text, with assistance
- Identify information that is implied rather than stated, with assistance

- Use self-monitoring strategies, such as cross-checking, summarizing, and self-questioning, to construct meaning of text
- Recognize when comprehension has been disrupted and initiate self-correction strategies, such as rereading, adjusting rate of reading, and attending to specific vocabulary
- Use knowledge of text structures to recognize and discriminate differences among a variety of texts and to support understanding
- Ask questions to clarify understanding and to focus reading
- Make connections between text being read and own lives, the lives of others, and other texts read in the past
- Use prior knowledge in concert with text information to support comprehension, from forming predictions to making inferences and drawing conclusions
- Read grade-level texts and answer literal, inferential, and evaluative questions
- State or summarize a main idea and support/elaborate with relevant details
- Present a point of view or interpretation of a text, such as

Standard 2: Students will read, write, listen, and speak for **literary response and expression.**

- Read, view, and interpret literary texts from a variety of genres
- Define characteristics of different genres
- Select literary texts on the basis of personal needs and interests and read silently for enjoyment for extended periods
- Read aloud from a variety of genres; for example, read the lines of a play or recite a poem
  - use inflection and intonation appropriate to text read and audience
- Recognize that the same story can be told in different genres, such as novels, poems, or plays, with assistance
- Identify literary elements, such as setting, plot, and character, of different genres
- Recognize how the author uses literary devices, such as simile, metaphor, and personification, to create meaning
- Recognize how different authors treat similar themes
- Identify the ways in which characters change and develop throughout a story
- Compare characters in literature to people in own lives

its theme, and support it with significant details from the text

- Participate cooperatively and collaboratively in group discussions of texts
- Note and describe aspects of the writer's craft
- Read aloud, accurately and fluently, with appropriate rate of reading, intonation, and inflection
- Demonstrate comprehension of grade-level texts through a range of responses, such as writing, drama, and oral presentations

Motivation to Read

- Show interest in a wide range of texts, topics, and genres for reading
- Read voluntarily for a variety of purposes
- Be familiar with titles and authors of a wide range of literature
- Engage in independent silent reading for extended periods of time

Standard 3: Students will read, write, listen, and speak for critical analysis and evaluation.

- Evaluate information, ideas, opinions, and themes in texts by identifying
  - a central idea and supporting details
  - details that are primary and those that are less important
  - statements of fact, opinion, and exaggeration
  - missing or unclear information
- Use established criteria to analyze the quality of information in text
- Identify different perspectives, such as social, cultural, ethnic, and historical, on an issue presented in one or more than one text

Standard 4: Students will read, write, listen, and speak for social interaction.

- Share reading experiences to build a relationship with peers or adults; for example, read together silently or aloud with a partner or in small groups
- Respect the age, sex, position, and cultural traditions of the writer
- Recognize conversational tone in friendly communication

	• Recognize the types of language (e.g., jargon, informal vocabulary, and e-mail conventions) that are appropriate to social communication

Grade 5 Writing

LITERACY COMPETENCIES	GRADE-SPECIFIC PERFORMANCE INDICATORS
The writing competencies common to all four ELA standards that students demonstrate during grade 5 are as follows:	The grade-specific performance indicators that grade 5 students demonstrate as they learn to write consist of the following:
Spelling	Standard 1: Students will read, write, listen, and speak for information and understanding.
• Correctly spell words within own writing that have been previously studied and/or frequently used	• Use at least three sources of information in writing a report, with assistance
• Correctly spell words within own writing that follow the spelling patterns of words that have been previously studied	• Take notes to record and organize relevant data, facts, and ideas, with assistance, and use notes as part of prewriting activities
• Spell a large body of words accurately and quickly when writing	• State a main idea and support it with details and examples
• Use a variety of spelling resources, such as spelling dictionaries and spell-check tools, to support correct spelling	• Compare and contrast ideas and information from two sources
	• Write labels or captions for graphics, such as charts, graphs,

Handwriting

- Use legible print and/or cursive writing

Composition

- Respond in writing to prompts that follow the reading of literary and informational texts
- Respond to writing prompts that follow listening to literary and informational texts
- Write on a wide range of topics
- Understand and use writing for a variety of purposes
- Use a variety of different organizational patterns for writing, such as chronological order, cause/effect, compare/contrast
- Use a variety of media, such as print and electronic, when writing
- Use the writing process (e.g., prewriting, drafting, revising, proofreading, and editing)
- Use a variety of prewriting strategies, such as brainstorming, freewriting, note taking, and webbing
- Review writing independently to revise for focus, development of ideas, and organization
- Review writing independently to edit for correct spelling, grammar, capitalization, punctuation, and paragraphing

and diagrams, to convey information

- Adopt an organizational format, such as chronological order, that is appropriate for informational writing
- Use paragraphing to organize ideas and information, with assistance
- Maintain a portfolio that includes informational writing

Standard 2: Students will read, write, listen, and speak for literary response and expression.

- Develop original literary texts that
  - use organizing structures such as stanzas and chapters
  - create a lead that attracts the reader's interest
  - provide a title that interests the reader
  - develop characters and establish a plot
  - use examples of literary devices, such as rhyme, rhythm, and simile
  - establish consistent point of view (e.g., first or third person) with assistance
- Write interpretive essays that
  - summarize the plot
  - describe the characters and how they change

- Understand and write for a variety of audiences
- Adjust style of writing, voice, and language used according to purpose and intended audience
- Incorporate aspects of the writer's craft, such as literary devices and specific voice, into own writing
- Use multiple sources of information when writing a report
- Review writing with teachers and peers

Motivation to Write

- Write voluntarily to communicate ideas and emotions to a variety of audiences, from self to unknown
- Write voluntarily for different purposes
- Write on a variety of topics
- Publish writing in a variety of presentation or display mediums, for a variety of audiences

- describe the setting and recognize its importance to the story
- draw a conclusion about the work
- interpret the impact of literary devices, such as simile and personification
- recognize the impact of rhythm and rhyme in poems
- Respond to literature, connecting the response to personal experience
- Use resources, such as personal experiences and themes from other texts and performances, to plan and create literary texts
- Maintain a writing portfolio that includes literary, interpretive, and responsive writing

Standard 3: Students will read, write, listen, and speak for **critical analysis and evaluation.**

- Use strategies, such as note taking, semantic webbing, or mapping, to plan and organize writing
- Use supporting evidence from text to evaluate ideas, information, themes, or experiences
- Analyze the impact of an event or issue from personal and peer group perspectives

- Analyze literary elements in order to evaluate the quality of ideas and information in text
- Use information and ideas from other subject areas and personal experiences to form and express opinions
- Adapt an organizational format, such as compare/contrast, appropriate for critical analysis and evaluation, with assistance
- Use precise vocabulary in writing analysis and evaluation, with assistance
- Maintain a writing portfolio that includes writing for critical analysis and evaluation

Standard 4: Students will read, write, listen, and speak for social interaction.

- Share the process of writing with peers and adults; for example, write a condolence note, get-well card, or thank-you letter with a writing partner or in small groups
- Respect the age, sex, position, and cultural traditions of the recipient
- Develop a personal voice that enables the reader to get to know the writer
- Write personal reactions to experiences and events, using a form of social communication

	• Maintain a portfolio that includes writing for social communication

Grade 5 Listening

LITERACY COMPETENCIES	GRADE-SPECIFIC PERFORMANCE INDICATORS
The listening competencies common to all four ELA standards that students demonstrate during grade 5 are as follows: Listening • Listen attentively to a variety of texts read aloud • Listen attentively for different purposes and for an extended period of time • Identify own purpose(s) for listening • Respond appropriately to what is heard • Listen respectfully, and without interrupting, when others speak.	The grade-specific performance indicators that grade 5 students demonstrate as they learn to listen consist of the following: Standard 1: Students will read, write, listen, and speak for information and understanding. • Follow instructions that provide information about a task or assignment • Identify essential details for note taking • Distinguish between fact and opinion • Identify information that is implicit rather than stated • Connect new information to prior knowledge or experience Standard 2: Students will read, write, listen, and speak for literary response and expression.

- Distinguish different genres, such as story, biography, poem, or play, with assistance
- Identify a character's motivation
- Recognize the use of literary devices, such as simile, personification, rhythm, and rhyme, in presentation of literary texts
- Use personal experience and prior knowledge to interpret and respond to literary texts and performances
- Identify cultural and historical influences in texts and performances, with assistance

Standard 3: Students will read, write, listen, and speak for critical analysis and evaluation.

- Form an opinion on a subject on the basis of information, ideas, and themes expressed in presentations
- Recognize and use the perspective of others to analyze presentations
- Use prior knowledge and experiences to analyze the content of presentations
- Recognize persuasive presentations and identify the techniques used to accomplish that purpose, with assistance
- Evaluate the quality of the speaker's presentation style by

using criteria such as volume, tone of voice, and rate

Standard 4: Students will read, write, listen, and speak for **social interaction.**

- Respect the age, sex, position, and cultural traditions of the speaker
- Recognize friendly communication on the basis of volume and tone of the speaker's voice
- Recognize that social communication may include informal language such as jargon
- Recognize the meaning of the speaker's nonverbal cues

Grade 5 Speaking

LITERACY COMPETENCIES	GRADE-SPECIFIC PERFORMANCE INDICATORS
The speaking competencies common to all four ELA standards that students demonstrate during grade 5 are as follows: Speaking • Speak in response to the reading of a variety of texts	The grade-specific performance indicators that grade 5 students demonstrate as they learn to speak include the following: **Standard 1:** Students will read, write, listen, and speak for **information and understanding.** • Ask probing questions

- Use appropriate and specific vocabulary to communicate ideas
- Use grammatically correct sentences when speaking
- Include details that are relevant for the audience
- Communicate ideas in an organized and coherent manner
- Vary the formality of language according to the audience and purpose for speaking
- Speak with expression, volume, pace, and gestures appropriate for the topic, audience, and purpose of communication
- Respond respectfully to others
- Participate in group discussions on a variety of topics
- Offer feedback to others in a respectful and responsive manner

- Interview peers
- Share information from personal experience
- Share information from a variety of texts
- State a main idea and support it with facts, details, and examples
- Compare and contrast information
- Present reports of approximately five minutes for teachers and peers
- Summarize main points
- Use notes, outlines, and visual aids appropriate to the presentation

Standard 2: Students will read, write, listen, and speak for literary response and expression.

- Present original works, such as stories, poems, and plays, to adults and peers, using audible voice and pacing appropriate to content and audience
- Share book reviews
- Summarize the plot and describe the motivation of characters
- Connect a personal response to literature to prior experience or knowledge
- Recognize the importance of cultural and historical characteristics in texts and performances

- Ask questions and respond to questions for clarification
- Use notes or outlines appropriately in presentations

Standard 3: Students will read, write, listen, and speak for critical analysis and evaluation.

- Ask questions and respond to questions for clarification
- Express an opinion about information, ideas, opinions, themes, and experiences in books, essays, articles, and advertisements
- Analyze an event or issue by using role play as a strategy
- Use information and ideas from personal experiences to form and express opinions and judgments
- Use notes or outlines appropriately in presentations

Standard 4: Students will read, write, listen, and speak for social interaction.

- Discuss the content of friendly notes, cards, and letters with a teacher or classmate in order to get to know the writer and each other
- Use the informal language of social communication
- Respect the age, sex, position, culture, and interests of the listener

- Use the rules of conversation, such as avoiding interrupting and responding respectfully

Courtesy New York State Education Department

Hermon R. Card (M.Ed.) is an English teacher, poet, educational consultant, and motivational speaker. He is also a museum educator at the National Baseball Hall of Fame and Museum. He has been a college baseball player and coach, military officer, tournament squash player, and NCAA baseball umpire.

He retired from his classroom position in July 2006 to devote his attention to his workshop/seminar series.

He has taught since 1974 in the Marcellus New York Central School District, and has presented professional development workshops, motivational seminars and poetry readings for some seventeen years. He is a New York State English Council *Educator of Excellence*, and his school's *Continual Celebration of Poetry*, which he developed in 1995, was designated a New York State English Council *Program of Excellence* in 2005.

He has worked in conjunction with the New York State Education Department and CTB/McGraw Hill on analyzing, reviewing, revising, and setting standards for New York ELA Assessment tests. He serves as a regional director on the board of the New York State English Council.

His most recent poetry book *…or else it's only a job,* was published in October 2006.

INDEX